MIRACLE AT CITY HALL

MIRACLE AT CITY HALL

by
Al Palmquist
with Kay Nelson

BETHANY FELLOWSHIP, INC.
Minneapolis, Minnesota

Photos by:
  Terry Dugan
  Ake Lundberg
  William Seaman

ISBN 0-87123-364-9
Library of Congress Catalog Card Number: 74-11738

Published by
BETHANY FELLOWSHIP, INC.
6820 Auto Club Road, Minneapolis, Minnesota 55438

Printed in the United States of America

FOREWORD

I met Al Palmquist during the 1973 Upper Midwest Billy Graham Crusade.

One of the nights during the Crusade, he testified to finding Christ at the 1961 Crusade.

Al is now the Director of Midwest Challenge and a Minneapolis police officer. His position is unique in that he is a police officer heading a Christian organization to rehabilitate drug addicts.

This book describes the unfolding of the miracle at City Hall which made the Center possible.

I know you will be thrilled at God's leading in Al's life as a Christian cop. You will ride the streets in his squad car, and relive with him the exciting experiences God put him through.

I wholeheartedly recommend *Miracle At City Hall* to you.

George Wilson
Executive Vice-President
Billy Graham Association

CHAPTER I

"Buy you a beer, Al?" asked Don as he lit another cigarette and teasingly blew the gray stream of smoke in my direction. Don didn't mind working the beat with a preacher turned cop, but he didn't let me forget it either.

"Or maybe a bottle of pop is more your style," he continued chuckling. "I'll buy, O.K.?"

"Man, get this paddy wagon moving," I replied jokingly. "You're such a cheap skate, you'll change your mind by the time we get there."

Pulling out of an alley, we headed for a gas station on 27th and Hennepin. It was Sunday morning and my partner and I had been cruising through the fifth precinct, looking for leftovers—dead bodies or stolen cars from the night before. There aren't many action calls on Sunday mornings; we spend most of our time beating the bush. The nasty people are either in jail or sleeping it off.

Slumping down in the seat, I put my knees against the dashboard. I was feeling a little nasty myself. Lately I had been depressed and that black mood hit hardest on Sundays. I felt close to God, but yet there was such an emptiness and frustration inside. It was as if I were supposed to be doing something in particular but just couldn't pinpoint what it was.

When I first started working on the police force, my expectations and dreams had seemed within reach. But it didn't take long to realize that the odds were against me. I had wanted to demonstrate Christ's love through a new medium—a policeman's uniform—never imagining that it would be the most difficult job I had ever tackled.

Now the possibility of having made a mistake nagged at me constantly. I had tried to love people, but little did I know how depraved people can become and what the effects of a steady diet of "dirt" could do to a person's attitudes and opinions. The churning revolution within my own personality was proof enough that God would have to do something out of the ordinary. And, if He didn't do something pretty soon, I would have to concede that I had presumed on God. After all, anyone could be doing the job I did, and he wouldn't have to be a Christian either.

Turning out of the traffic, my partner interrupted. "What are you thinking so hard about?" he asked as he pulled up next to the gas station.

"That bottle of pop you promised me," I replied, not wanting him to bug me anymore. "Let's go."

Getting out of the squad car, I reached over and turned up the car radio loud enough so we wouldn't miss a call. It was getting towards ten o'clock in the morning, and the day was already hot and sticky.

Under my breath I said a quick prayer. "Dear God, please don't let it rain today." I had promised Gayle I would play tennis with her after work. She was a good wife and very seldom complained, but even wives need attention sometimes.

8

In fact, when I first joined the force I had told Gayle how great it was going to be just to work an eight-hour shift. In New York where I had worked with Teen Challenge, there had never been a minute I could completely call my own unless I left town. Even in the middle of the night some "junkie" would try to cut out, or needed counseling, and we had to be available.

After I left Teen Challenge I was sure I would have more time for my wife, my children, and especially the Lord. However, court cases and extra jobs soon began to encroach on my time to the point that my spiritual life was "on the run" too. Only one idea, one prayer remained constant: "Lord, meet the needs of those I work with—on both sides of the law."

"Hey, the pop machine is over here, Al," called Don as I shut the car door. As he motioned to me, he headed towards the opposite side of the building.

Stretching my gait to catch up, I rounded the back end of a blue Chevy parked between us and the vending machine. I walked past the open window and then, retracing my steps, I felt as if a little alarm had gone off inside me. The motor was running but there were no keys in the ignition.

"Who owns this car?" I yelled. I had noticed three fellows with a "just-not-right" look about them, sitting inside the station. They apparently were hashing over some problem and were divided two against one.

"It's my friend's," answered one of the three, trying to ignore me as I looked him over. He appeared to be about twenty to twenty-two years old, medium height, and skinny. His blond hair hung like a mop over his deep-set blue eyes, half hiding the dark shadows circling his lids.

Blond, blue-eyed Scandinavians aren't uncommon in Minneapolis, but the long-sleeved brown wool shirt along with filthy blue denim cut-offs seemed a little strange for this weather.

Convinced that this was only the beginning of lies, I continued, "What's his name?"

"I don't know. It's just some guy that let me use it." About this time the others were trying to stifle their snickering and I was sensing that special quiver of excitement inside when you've got something.

While my partner continued the questioning, I hurried back to the car and contacted the dispatcher. His job is to feed our information and questions into a computer down at City Hall and then return the needed information.

"Squad 550," I said, turning down the radio so I wouldn't get my ear blasted off when he answered.

"550 go ahead."

"I want a QMR on 9RF222."

Within thirty seconds the dispatcher had returned to the air saying the computer indicated the blue Chevy to be a stolen St. Paul vehicle.

"O.K. I'm booking one from 27th and Hennepin. Send a booking tow for 9RF222."

By this time the station attendant was getting a little nervous. A customer had pulled in, smelled trouble and headed out, not bothering to stop. Now he was standing behind the till, trying to look inconspicuous, yet not wanting to miss any of the action.

Returning from the squad I nodded at Don. He had been studying my face and was usually able to guess the right verdict without much difficulty.

"O.K., you've lied enough," he said, "You're under arrest." The fellow had been smoking nervously before. Now the color drained from his face, while

10

his "friends" began to edge slowly toward the door.

"And the computer doesn't lie," I added matter-of-factly. "You other guys had better clear out fast."

As I carefully handcuffed the kid's hands behind his back, Don searched him for possible weapons and identification. After finding his identification papers, we checked with the Hennepin County Warrant Office for a possible warrant. He was wanted for forgery. There weren't any smart answers now, and he winced as I tightened the irons on his wrists.

"Let's go," snapped Don, grabbing him by the arm and shoving him towards the car.

Walking beside him, I could see reflected in his sullen face the seething hatred he felt for cops and probably society in general. When we got to the squad car, my partner got into the driver's seat while I opened the back door.

"I'm not going anywhere, Cop," he snarled, his body stiffening like a ramrod. It's pretty hard to get somebody into the back seat of a car when he's decided to resist, so I finally pushed the kid's neck down and gave him a forceful shove in. He landed in a heap and didn't bother getting up.

There wasn't much traffic on the way downtown that morning, so I spent the time filling out the arrest report. This was the part of police work that I disliked the most. It was only for the sake of conscience that I didn't try to push it off on my partner more often.

Occasionally I glanced over my shoulder through the screen that separates the front from the back seat in all police cars. The kid was still lying sprawled out on the seat, but he had begun to moan periodically, glancing furtively around the back as if expecting someone to jump him any second.

By the time we arrived at City Hall, we had to

physically drag him out of the car and carry him down the steps into the building. City Hall is a monstrous, drab, dark brown building which covers a full city block. It has stone walls several feet thick and reminds one of an ancient castle surrounded by a moat. Police headquarters and its various divisions are located on ground floor, with the jail on fourth floor.

Passing homicide and the juvenile division, we headed for the jail elevator.

"Take us to the penthouse, Jo," I said, as we lifted the limp kid into the elevator. His chalky color and nervous twitching were beginning to get on my nerves.

"What's the matter with him?" asked Jo, who usually paid little attention to what went on inside the elevator.

"I don't know," I sighed. "I guess he's not too happy about going to jail." Actually I was wondering myself. This guy had looked tough when we first saw him, and I was sure this wasn't the first time he'd had a run-in with the law.

Seconds later the elevator opened and we were faced with a mass of iron doors and bars. An electronically controlled buzzer sounded and, pushing the iron gate open, we walked in.

The first thing we do when we get upstairs is to check our guns into a special locker. Many people get more violent when they see all the bars up there and would make trouble for us if they ever got hold of a gun. By the time we got to the booking desk, the prisoner wasn't in any shape to be answering questions; so I handed his identification papers to the sheriff. All of a sudden I heard an awful wretching sound and felt a warm, wet gush on the back of my left arm. The kid was doubled over, throwing up all over the floor—and me.

"Palmquist, help me carry this slob back to the cell," the deputy sheriff said. "We'll fingerprint him later. Got enough work around here without having to mop floors, too."

Grabbing his arms, we dragged him down the hall and dumped him into the nearest empty cell. As I opened the paint-chipped bars, the dirty gray cement floor seemed to jump up at me, grabbing the four-by-six cell in a cold, damp clutch.

"I'm going back to the desk. You can lock him up, Palmquist."

"O.K., let's get those clothes off," I began. It was getting late and I wanted to get out of there. Walking over to help him, I grabbed a shirt sleeve and started pulling it off. That's when the pieces began fitting together. There were tracks up and down both arms, looking like a map of the interstate highways all marked in red. This guy was a "junkie," and I had walked around like an idiot all morning, not recognizing his condition! It was no wonder he was vomiting. He suddenly realized that jail meant the end of his drug supply.

"Have you ever tried to get off drugs, kid?"

"Look, Fuzz, I've tried every lousy program in Minnesota," he sneered.

"Well, what would you think about a religious program?" I continued, wondering just how far to push the issue. I wasn't sure if he could handle the concern and love that overwhelmed me in that second. "I used to work at a place called Teen Challenge in New York City," I added, trying to encourage him, "and most of the fellows that came there shook the habit."

I told him that fellows had come into the center completely enslaved to hard narcotics but through earnestly committing their lives to Jesus Christ in prayer, they were able to begin a new life. The guilt that secretly hung so heavily on their consciences disappeared, and being freed, they were motivated to please the One who did for them what no human could do. I told him that this personal relationship with God was the source and sustenance of their new life.

"I know God is the only One who can help me," he interrupted. He had been staring at the floor while I talked. Now he shifted his eyes to me. "Isn't there some program like that around here?"

I felt the color creep up my neck as I looked into his expectant, pleading eyes. Why hadn't I kept my big mouth shut!

Groping for an answer, I thought of Dave. *If only Wilkerson were here in Minneapolis. It would be easy to get something going then. He seemed to have faith to spare.* But I felt like the guy in the Bible who was going around saying, "Go in peace. Be warmed and fed." And yet he sent people away hungry and empty-handed.

"Look, man," I stammered, wanting to say something encouraging and yet realistic.

"Get lost, Pig!" he screamed, pounding the wall with his fists. I had suggested a "new bag" to him, but he had found it full of hot air.

Hurriedly I locked the cell while the full force of my job hit me again. It was one thing to shut jail doors, but I didn't know how much longer I could keep it up without having a chance to open a few.

Discouraged and frustrated, I couldn't hold back the tears any longer as I walked down the hall. I wanted to escape his piercing screams as quickly as possible, but where could I go? It seemed as if God had put a roadblock in front of me every time I opened my mouth. Angry and defeated I unloaded my bitterness. "God," I questioned, "why do I get this far and no further? Either do something or get me out of this job."

"What's wrong with you?" asked Don, who had been standing near the gun locker talking to one of the deputy sheriffs.

"Not much," I mumbled as I picked up my gun. I wasn't embarrassed in front of Don. He had seen me "up-tight" before, but he also knew that I was no softy. Fresh out of police academy, I had saved his neck one night in a street action with a huge lumberjack from northern Minnesota.

It had been raining and the ground was terribly slippery. As I came out of an alley onto Franklin Avenue, I saw this great big six-foot-eight-inch guy beating up two policemen outside of a bar. One cop was already on the ground and Don was on his way down. Slamming on the brakes, I skidded to a stop. Being six foot three inches tall, my long legs helped me cover ground quite quickly. So, before he could untangle himself from the other cop, I jumped into the air as if grabbing for a rebound in basketball; and snagging a fistful of hair from behind, I pulled him backwards, causing him to trip over his own big feet. A few seconds later, the partner I was riding with at that time showed up and immobilized him with Mace, a chemical tear gas.

Later, after getting him into the squad car, one of the officers who had been down came over to me and said, "Wow! Thanks, Preach." It wasn't long before the story got around that I had single-handedly "thumped" this guy.

As I pushed the elevator button, the clang of the last big iron gate reechoed in my ears and scraped the edges of my nerves. On the way down, my mind flashed back fifteen years to another time when I

15

had listened to and felt that same sound. However, the gate had been closed on me that time.

As a teen-ager I had been involved in a Minneapolis gang called the Musketeers. One of our extracurricular activities was stealing. Add to this a merry-go-round of gambling, fights, drinking and wild parties, and my weekly routine was set.

I had become so adept at thieving that it became a game—that is, until I got busted. I didn't spend much time behind bars because I was still a juvenile, but the experience started me thinking.

The next summer I attended a Billy Graham Crusade in Minneapolis. It was an experience that shook me from head to foot. As I committed my life to Jesus Christ, I felt the peace of God flow through my body; and the weight of all the sins and hate which had consumed me just rolled off, leaving me free and whole.

The elevator slowed and jerked to a stop, and so did my revery. It was late and Gayle would be looking for me.

Retracing our steps past juvenile and homicide divisions, Don and I headed up the stairs toward the squad car which was parked on the west side of City Hall. We got into the car and headed south. It looked like rain. The weather had cooled off and clouded over; and we still had to get back to the fifth precinct house and check out before I could get home.

Driving along, I thought about Gayle. She had always said I would never rest until I got a program going to help "junkies" in the Minneapolis area. And deep down inside I knew that she was right. The only problem was how?

CHAPTER II

"Andrews, Dawson, Jamieson, Lark..." The monotonous drone of Sergeant Erickson's voice continued as the last of the stragglers filed into the precinct house. It was the end of September and I shivered from the early morning chill.

"Psst... Palmquist," whispered Oliveri, nudging me as we came to attention. "I've got to talk to you. Meet me in the hall after roll call. It's important."

"Shut your fat mouths, you guys," snapped Erickson, irked by the interruption. "Haven't you got any respect for the brass? You can solve your problems later."

"Sorry," I mumbled, snapping to attention. I didn't know for sure what Oliveri wanted, but I had a pretty good inkling.

During the past summer in fifth precinct, I had tried to refocus on the drug problem in Minneapolis. Each time I had met up with a drug addict, I had tried to visualize him as a whole person—the product of a program that only existed in my mind. I tried to imagine myself putting an arm around him and saying, "Come on. God loves you and I'll help you." But each time I had to ask myself, "With what?" I knew it wasn't enough to say, "Come to my church." I had to provide a bed, food, clothing and a job as well.

I couldn't see any possible way of starting a program by myself, nor were there enough spare hours in the day to get personally involved with junkies. So I started dropping little pieces of my dream in the ears of those I worked with.

Little by little, I had seen several cops warm up to the possibility of helping addicts. Many cops believe that the only good addict is a dead one; but these guys had begun to realize that the things they were seeing and experiencing on the street could not be explained in physical terms alone.

One of the fellows I unloaded on was Mike Oliveri. Mike was a six-foot, dark-haired, good-looking Italian who had started rooky school the same time that I had.

It wasn't long after we entered the academy until I realized that Mike was a Christian. Every time an instructor told a dirty joke during a lecture, the whole class would laughingly turn around to watch the color climb up old "pizza belly's" neck. There was no doubt in the minds of the others where Oliveri stood. He was an outspoken witness to the police force—and respected for it.

During lunch breaks most of the rookies spent their time playing cards or shooting crap. Mike and I talked about how we would handle ourselves on the street. Some of the officers liked to drop remarks about two other preachers who had been on the force before. Apparently they were real softies, and we were determined to drop that tag without losing our Christian reputation.

As we neared the end of our training, one of the brass in charge of the police academy, a twenty-year veteran, developed blood clots in his legs. He was really up-tight about the possibility of losing a leg or two, and everybody felt the tension when he was around.

One day during lunch Mike turned to me with his dogmatic voice and announced, "Look, Al, I think you had better tell the inspector we're going to pray for him and God will heal him."

"Me?" I choked, spilling my pop as I set it down. I knew there was no use arguing with Oliveri. Very few people were ever able to change his mind—and then with a lot of difficulty. But I just wasn't prepared to get up and march into the inspector's office and state God's case.

"Hey, wait a minute," I said. "It seems a little more reasonable that we flip a coin or something. O.K.?"

He agreed and five minutes later I was walking into the inspector's office. "Excuse me, sir," I stammered.

"What do you want?" he asked, continuing to stare out the window, his back towards me.

"Ah . . . Mike and I want you to know that we're concerned; and we're going to pray for you and also get our churches to pray for you." My heart was pounding in my ears as I continued. "We believe God can——"

"Heal me?" he interrupted, swinging his swivel chair around to face me. "Thank you, Palmquist." As he said this the tears began to roll down his cheeks.

Afraid that he might be embarrassed in front of me, I hurriedly turned around and left. But God didn't. Those clots dissolved and the inspector is still walking around on two good legs.

Until that incident I really didn't know just how committed Mike actually was. He had been a polite listener at first, but somewhat cool when I related some of the happenings I had experienced in New York City. However, as I continued to describe the work at Teen Challenge, I noticed a growing concern and excitement in his response. Lately he had been thinking about taking a year's leave of absence to work at Teen Challenge in New York, but he couldn't seem to make up his mind.

During college Oliveri had studied for the ministry, but in the last semester of his senior year, newly married and needing money, he joined the police force. After he graduated he just stayed on. The pay was good and so were the benefits; but gradually he realized he didn't belong. Now he was trying to find out just where he did belong.

I was so involved thinking about Oliveri that I was unaware of grunting my usual response to roll call until my partner, Don, commented on the way out. "You working today, Palmquist, or are you going to spend the day praying?"

Grabbing my hat, I headed for the squad car. Mike was already waiting for me in the hall. "I've decided to give it a try, Al," he blurted out first thing. "Jim Robertson said he'd go along with me to talk to the chief tomorrow." Jim was a Christian policeman who worked in the planning and research department at City Hall. "I want you to be there too. It will take all the help I can get. How about it?" he asked, turning to walk alongside of me.

The next day was my day off and I had planned on staying home; but Mike and I had begun to confide a lot in each other, and I didn't want to let him down. "O.K.," I replied. "I'll meet you in Robertson's office about ten tomorrow morning."

"What's with him?" asked Don as I got into the squad car. "Oh, he just wants me to help him with something tomorrow," I replied, trying to stifle a yawn as I stretched my arms. Most of the other officers had downed a couple of cups of coffee by now, but being a "teetotaler" it took me a long while to wake up in the morning, especially when it was chilly.

Pulling away from the curb, we headed the squad car toward Franklin Avenue. Our district was from Franklin to 38th Street South and Lyndale Avenue to St. Louis Park on the west. Besides being one of the busiest areas in the city, it was also unique.

Nearly 50,000 single people lived in the apartment houses on the east side. A lot of them were "junkies" and "long hairs." While the straight guys were working regular jobs during the day, the addicts burglarized the apartments. At night when everybody had time to kill, it turned into the biggest party area in Minneapolis.

It wasn't unusual to wrap up an assault case and fifteen minutes later be called to a burglary several blocks west in a wealthy residential area. This section of the beat included Lake Calhoun, Lake of the Isles, and Cedar Lake—all surrounded by $60,000 to $70,000 homes. Running through the middle of both areas was Lake Street, a heavy business district and impromptu drag strip.

By lunch time we had covered the entire area several times, circling block after block, studying people and cars. Inside the squad car Don and I made small talk as we listened to the noisy chatter of the radio.

The day was slow and we didn't do much other than write a few traffic tickets until about 2:30 p.m.

when our call number was put on the air.

"550 . . . 550. What is your location?"

"Main beach Calhoun," I said, picking up the mike.

"There's a complaint from 2501 Grand Avenue. Somebody's trying to kill a woman with an axe. Got it?"

"Copy. We're on our way." Making a quick U-turn, we threw on the siren and headed for Grand Avenue, screaming down the street at breakneck speed. As we neared the address, Don pulled out of the traffic, turning off the red light and siren. Contrary to the TV programs, we didn't want this guy to know we were coming.

When we arrived at the house, a group of people came charging towards the car shouting at us in Spanish. No one was giving the other guy a chance to talk; but having worked with Spanish-speaking people in New York, I was able to make out a few words in all the confusion. The suspect was a man; he headed south, carried an axe, and wore a yellow shirt and green pants. Apparently the victim wasn't a victim at all. Just scared!

As the frantic group carried on with their gyrations, we drove south looking for someone in a yellow shirt and green pants. Three blocks later we found him, standing in front of the large bay window of a residential home, his nose pressed against the pane while he rubbed his hands around in circles on the glass. He reminded me of someone trying to develop coordination by rubbing his stomach and patting his head at the same time, but doing a pretty poor job of it.

Pulling my gun, I walked up behind him unnoticed and said, "Hey, put your hands straight up in the air and turn around quick." The axe was leaning against his leg, and I was hoping he'd knock it over as he turned around.

Halfway around he stopped, stared at me with an emotionless look and whimpered, "That guy won't give me any rootbeer."

"What guy?" I asked, cautiously working my way towards him. I wanted to keep his attention so Don could get hold of the axe.

"The rootbeer guy in there," he replied, pointing to an old man who was peering out from behind the drapes. "He's the one who won't give me any rootbeer."

"Isn't that too bad. The guy must be prejudiced."

"Yeah," he sighed as if talking to an old friend. By this time I was sure he was taking a trip on LSD or he'd probably have called me "pig" and every other dirty cop word he could think of. But now he figured I was the one to help him get some rootbeer.

"Hey, I'll take you to the big rootbeer man up in the sky," I laughed, referring to the fourth floor jail in City Hall. How about it?"

While he was thinking it over I added, "Let me put these pretty bracelets on you first. They'll keep you out of trouble."

Several minutes later he actually seemed happy as we headed downtown. However, he couldn't forget about that rootbeer and kept asking us for some every few seconds.

That night I had a good laugh when I told Gayle about the "rootbeer" adventure. However, it didn't seem so funny the next morning as I drove down to meet Mike and Jim Robertson. I wondered if maybe God hadn't viewed the situation quite as lightly as I had!

Jim had set up a meeting for us with Gordon

Johnson, chief of police, and it was my duty to sell him on the idea of letting Oliveri get further training at Teen Challenge. Hopefully, he would return to the force a much wiser and more effective cop, particularly with drug addicts.

Just thinking about it made me nervous. I had never met the chief before, nor did I figure he'd be very interested in my opinions or suggestions, especially since I had a deficit on seniority. Besides, I wasn't sure the idea was all that good. I certainly didn't feel effective with all that training. And, yesterday's incident just reemphasized to me how big the problem was and how little my influence on it amounted to.

Turning into the police garage I parked the car, signed in, and headed upstairs. As I hurried through the tunnel, I felt dry-mouthed and weak-kneed. Leaving the rumbling echo of my footsteps behind, I hurried up two flights of stairs and found Oliveri in Robertson's office looking nervously at his watch. It was 9:59 and the chief expected people to be on time, particularly police officers.

"Come on, let's go talk," said Robertson, heading for the door. Within seconds we had crossed the hall and were being ushered into the chief's office.

"Chief," began Robertson, skipping the preliminaries, "Oliveri would like a year's leave of absence to work at Teen Challenge in New York. What do you think?" The chief had been looking at Jim, shifted his glance to Mike, and finally settled on me.

"Well, Palmquist, I hear you were in New York for a while," he began. "How do you like being back in the Midwest?"

"Well, sir," I said, clearing my throat and sitting a little forward in my seat. I wanted my answer to make a good impression, but before I could organize my thoughts he continued.

"How do you feel about the police force, having been a preacher and all?"

About that time I was beginning to get a little uneasy. He seemed to be probing for something, and the way he looked at me reminded me of another interview I had had when I first applied for the police job.

Everyone entering the police academy is required to take the Minnesota Multiphasic Test—a psychiatric test used to screen applicants. A lot of people want to be a policeman for one reason or the other. And it's these "other reason" people that don't make good cops and usually don't get accepted.

When I applied for the force an employee in the civil service department told me that two thousand people had applied and only forty-two were being accepted. That's why when the staff psychiatrist set up an appointment for me, I was pretty sure my ambitions were short-lived.

I had also had a run-in with a female instructor a few days earlier during sensitivity training. Before she began her first lecture she proceeded to introduce herself. "I used to be a Baptist," she began, "but now I'm a Christian." A half a breath later she was spewing out a line of filthy language at an inattentive cop in the back row.

Instantly I snapped my arm up in the air and without thinking said the first thing that came to my mind, "I doubt that you were ever a Baptist. And, you certainly aren't a Christian. As for being a lady . . . no way!"

The class roared with laughter as I began to imagine the repercussions of my outburst. And, as I walked down the hall toward the psychiatrist's office, my imagination continued to work overtime. The instructor had really been angry. I could sense she intended to make trouble for me.

Entering his office, I noticed that the shades were down and two big comfortable armchairs were drawn up close to each other. Apparently he wanted me to relax so I could give him the "right" answers.

"I see here that you have been to Bible school, Mr. Palmquist," he said, trying his best to appear serious. It was obvious he thought he was going to have some fun with me. "Do you pray every day?"

"Ah . . . yes, I do," I replied, somewhat off guard. His direct approach surprised me. I had expected him to draw the answers out of me more subtly.

"I have a few questions I'd like to ask you, Mr. Palmquist," he continued, pausing only a second. "What would you do if you had to kill somebody?"

I was glad I had recently heard a pastor speak on this subject, so I just repeated his explanation. "I believe the fifth commandment, 'thou shalt not kill,' would be better translated, 'thou shalt do no murder,' " I began. "You see, the word murder implies hate and animosity, whereas the word kill does not always imply the same feelings. This at least gives me a loophole for duty," I said, watching to see what his expression would be.

"Just one more question," he continued, raising his left eyebrow just slightly. "Why do you want to be a cop?"

By this time it was obvious that I had scored too highly in religious overtones on the M.M.T. And, I knew what kind of response he was hoping for—like, "I feel it's God's will," or some other typical cliche. I really did feel it was God's plan for my life at this time, but I knew I couldn't tell him or he'd label me crazy and have plenty of reason to recommend I not be accepted. Finally, putting on my most refined and sober look, I answered, "Well, since I'm half Irish and a flat-foot to start with, I think cop work is my bag."

This seemed to be the turning point in our conversation. A while later he was still chuckling as I walked out the door, but his chuckle didn't have any antagonistic overtones.

And, as Chief Johnson continued to discuss Mike's leave of absence with Jim, it was obvious that his attitude also was neither cold nor indifferent. Suddenly he turned to me again and commented, "Don't you think we ought to have a program like Teen Challenge in Minneapolis, Palmquist? Maybe you ought to start one."

Stunned—I sat there, torn between the churning excitement I felt and the nagging fear that kept me from saying anything. Did he really know what he was suggesting? Was a sophisticated law force about to endorse Christ's love as the most effective deterrent to crime? Could the church and the police department actually work together?

The sudden anticipation and joy I felt wanted to shout, "Yes, Yes!" But could I be sure? Was he really serious or was he just trying to include me in the conversation?

The next thing I knew, the chief and Jim Robertson were wrapping up the details of Oliveri's leave of absence and we were being ushered out.

As the door clicked shut the excitement I sensed gained momentum. Grabbing Jim, I asked, "Was he serious?"

"Look, Palmquist," he said, grinning rather knowledgeably. "When he says something, he means it. But I'll find out for sure."

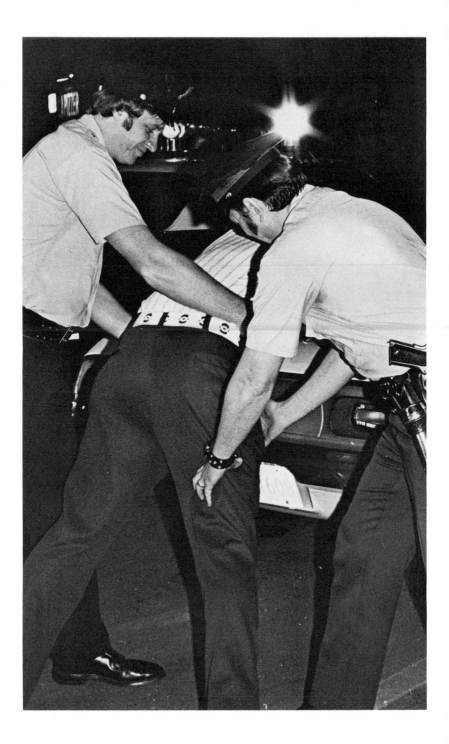

CHAPTER III

It was a blustery cold October morning when the telephone rang. It had been exactly two weeks since Jim had promised to check with Chief Johnson about some kind of drug program through the police department.

During these two weeks I had continually mulled the idea over in my mind, pitting logic against daydreams. As a policeman I had to approach the situation logically. Drug addiction was a crime in itself, let alone the burglary, mugging and murder that often accompanied it. The police department had a job to do and a public to satisfy. Many people were already complaining that criminals were getting off too easily. This might appear to be just another gimmick to some people.

In spite of this, however, I sensed an expectancy— as if God were about to do something special. I didn't know what it would be, but still I was excited about the possibility of being involved in it. There was only one question that continued to haunt me. If City Hall really did initiate a drug program, would junkies want to get involved with cops, even if they were trying to help them?

The logic usually raised more problems than I could dream away; so, one day, after I had bugged Gayle with these difficulties night and day for more than a week, she remarked, "Look, honey, why don't you relax a bit and just wait and see if anything happens? You've always got so many big ideas and then in a few days you forget about them."

I guess that's why I was caught off guard that morning when she reached across the kitchen table to hand me the telephone.

"Hello, . . . Mr. Palmquist?" asked a rather high-pitched cracking voice. "This is the mayor's office calling. What are you doing?"

"I'm eating breakfast," I began, wondering what was going on. It sounded as if someone was laughing in the background; and whoever was on the other end of the receiver was searching for something to say next.

Obviously someone was trying to pull my leg, so I asked, "Who is this?" Figuring it was Jim Robertson, I continued, "Is that you Robertson, you old ding-a-ling?"

"How are you doing, man?" he asked. His tone was more serious now. "All kidding aside, Al, can you come down to City Hall this morning about eleven o'clock? The mayor wants to talk to you."

"About what?" I asked as the excitement mounted within me.

"Wait and see," he replied jokingly. "I'm sure it will be of interest to you!" Jim was a great sport and liked to tease, even when he was helping a guy out.

"O.K. I'll be there."

As I hung up the telephone, I felt like tossing

logic out the window. My dreams began to mushroom as I remembered a statement made by Mayor Stenvig when he first took office: "God is my boss. I'll take my orders from Him."

The news media had made a big stir about this statement, but as I sat staring out the window I wanted to rely on those words. I didn't know if they were true or not, but if God was really giving orders to the mayor, it would be evident in the days ahead.

Gulping the last of my orange juice, I felt a surge of satisfaction and expectation that I hadn't sensed since I left Brooklyn. If these new feelings weren't leading into a cul-de-sac, I would soon be readjusting my life patterns again as well as trying to reconstruct the lives of others.

A hundred memories flooded my mind as I reflected on previous lives that I had touched. One of them was a guy named Torri. Torri was one of those who just couldn't seem to do anything right. In fact, that was the main complaint against him as the staff met for evaluations. He had been at the center more than three weeks and although the counselors tried their best, he didn't respond to their efforts or innovations, new or old. He was sullen and secretive, and quite often he refused to get involved in the activities.

As his chart was discussed, most of the staff agreed that he should leave. Torri had given me trouble, too, but I still didn't want to kick him out. Maybe he reminded me of myself or something, but I knew he needed one more chance.

"Give Torri a couple more days," I had requested. "I'm sure I can get through to him."

The next day we bussed the fellows to a meeting on the Lower East Side. We had rented the East Side Theater House, a run-down delapidated building located in one of the worst slum areas of New York City. By the looks of it I was convinced that the first movie ever produced had been shown there. All afternoon we had canvassed the area, inviting people to attend the meeting. Now, as we entered the auditorium, I noticed a cross-section of people—some from as far away as Long Island and New Jersey, some from the lower income housing projects, and then the fellows from the center. As we sat there, waiting for Dave Wilkerson to begin speaking, the air hung heavy with a combination of body odors and musty smells from seats and draperies.

In the confusion around me, I prayed. I didn't have time to win Torri's confidence nor the ability to convince him that Christ could take care of whatever was bugging him, so I asked God for a miracle.

And I got one. Before the evening was over, Torri had committed his past and future to Jesus Christ. He left that building a different person, free from the guilt of past crimes and hoping for a chance to start over.

A few days later Torri approached me. He was discouraged and worried. He wanted to unload on someone but wasn't sure what would happen if he did. Finally, he broke down and told me the whole story.

Torri's reason for entering the Teen Challenge program hadn't been exactly pure. It was more a matter of convenience than desire for help. He had failed to keep parole, and one day while walking through the Bedford Stuyvesant area in Brooklyn his parole officer spotted him. Trying to escape, Torri took to the rooftops. Leaping and running from one building to another, he finally found himself looking into a fenced-in backyard. Lots of people were milling around; so, he just joined the crowd. Later, he realized that he was in some kind of drug rehabilitation center and decided to hide out there.

Now, having rejected the dishonesty of his past life, he felt he must leave the center and turn himself in. I knew if Torri left the center alone, the pressures of his old environment would be too much for him; so I suggested that I go along to see his parole officer. I was sure we could explain everything to him and trust God to bring Torri back to the center.

As we walked in the door, I felt my heart skip a beat. Torri's parole officer was one of the biggest, meanest looking black guys I had ever seen. Grabbing Torri, he slammed him up against the wall, knocking his red-covered Bible out of his coat pocket.

"What kind of con-game you playing now, Torrino?" he asked, looking down at the Bible lying open on the floor. "Turned preacher, no doubt! Let's check out those arms, baby," he continued. "Take off your coat."

When he saw that there were no fresh tracks on Torri's arms, he turned to me with a puzzled look and asked, "Who are you?"

Taking the opportunity, I introduced myself and explained why I was there and what had happened to Torri since he skipped parole. The parole officer sat there listening intently and then, turning to face Torri squarely, he said, "Torrino, you're the first junkie I've ever seen that might make it."

And, Torri did make it. After he finished the rehabilitation program, he applied for further schooling and eventually became a preacher of the Gospel. God had transformed his life, his thinking, and his ambitions.

Thinking about ambition, I figured I had better start pursuing my own. The minutes were flying by and I still had to get dressed. Gayle and I usually ate a late breakfast whenever I was supposed to start the night shift. That's why I had been lounging around in pajamas all that morning.

Hurriedly I slipped into slacks and a shirt. I could make better time, I figured, if I took Park Avenue down to 3rd Street and then cut over. I had headed towards City Hall from so many directions while working on the police force that I had begun to think of City Hall as the center of my little world.

Walking towards the door I called back to Gayle. "Good-bye, honey. I'll see you later."

"Hey, wait a minute, Al," she said, running out of the bedroom with a sport coat on her arm. "Don't you think you should at least put a coat on?" she asked. "It isn't exactly as if you were going to play golf."

Taking the coat from her, I put my arms around Gayle and held her close. I could tell that she was anxious for me and wanted me to make a good impression. I didn't mind, and I rather doubted that God cared either, if I tried to help Him out a little by looking sharp.

Kissing her lightly on the lips, I headed for the car. Mechanically I started the motor and pulled into the traffic. Usually I listened to Christian music on the tape deck as I drove along, but this morning I didn't bother turning it on. I felt such a compelling urge to get some definite guidance from God. What if the mayor asked me to start a program and then set up regulations that opposed the freedom we needed to preach the Gospel? What if he insisted that the staff be professionals—psychiatrists, social workers, etc.?

A few weeks ago I had asked God to get the right people involved in this project—that is, if there was going to be a project—and now I was pretty sure that the mayor was one of them. However, I didn't want the program to have political strings attached to it. It needed the power that can only be provided by a spiritual encounter with God.

I had visited several secular drug programs since returning to Minneapolis and, although I appreciated the effort they were making, it seemed to me that those who made use of these facilities were still hung up on something, whether it was Methadon or another substitute.

I knew God was the only one who could free from drugs and then fill the empty void that was left, so I prayed as I drove along, trusting God to control and energize this project. Jim was waiting for me as I entered his office.

"Hi . . . what's up?" I asked, straddling the straight-back desk chair and leaning forward.

"Don't get too comfortable! You've got a meeting with the chief and Mayor Stenvig," he replied. "We'd better get going before you're late."

Jim stood behind the desk, his intense blue eyes shining. He was one of the most gregarious souls I had ever met. Twelve years ago he had joined the police force because he liked people but wanted to avoid sales quotas and marketing. Now it seemed that everyone liked him. He was one of the biggest blessings on the force.

Jim also shared the same philosophy about drug addiction that I did, and I often felt more comfortable just knowing that he was on my side.

I had been hoping that Jim would be at the meeting in the mayor's office also, but he mumbled something about lots of paper work to do and left. Standing alone with Chief Johnson, I waited for him to make the next move. A few seconds later he got up and headed for the back door, motioning for me to follow him. As we walked down the hall to the mayor's office, silence reigned.

The reception room was empty. The chief walked past the mayor's private secretary and opened the door to the inner office. I was close behind, but as I approached the secretary's desk she stood up and forcefully spread her presence in my path. At fifty she was slightly grey and well rounded, so that I wouldn't have been able to get past her even if I had dared.

"Who are you and where do you think you're going?" she demanded. Her voice reminded me of cold winter winds.

"I'm with the chief," I stammered, hoping he'd turn around and rescue me. I was beginning to feel my insignificance around the place. If there was ever anything to be done, God was going to have to be out in front. I couldn't even get past the mayor's secretary, even when I was obviously accompanied by the chief of police.

"We're together," commented the chief, glancing over his shoulder at my awkward position.

Inside the office the chief introduced me to the mayor. Standing next to him, I was at least six inches taller, but for a few seconds I felt like a little jelly bean. The large dark brown paneled room was carpeted in a lush green, giving it a severe yet cool look. A massive mahogany desk faced the door, while a large conference table, big enough to seat about fifteen people, was located on the right.

As Mayor Stenvig sat down behind his desk, I lowered myself into a large overstuffed easy chair, feeling smaller and smaller as I sank deeper into the layers of foam.

Turning to the chief, the mayor began, "Well,

Gordon, what do you think of this idea?" From the puzzled look on the chief's face I could tell that they had discussed this matter previously. "I can see that your mind is already made up," he continued. Switching his attention from Johnson to me he added, "If the chief is for you, I am too, Palmquist. I've read several of Wilkerson's books and I'm convinced that a drug program without Christ doesn't have the answer."

"How do you want me to put the thing together?" I asked, beginning to feel a load of responsibility settle in on me.

"I'm the mayor, you're the preacher," he chuckled. "The only advice I've got is no government grants. We don't want to push God out the back door."

He was right, of course, and I knew it. But still I wondered where all the money was going to come from as I listened to the mayor cut off all those political strings that I had prayed about. At Teen Challenge the money had come in in miraculous ways, but then Wilkerson also had a bit of charisma that I lacked.

After shaking hands with the mayor, the chief and I walked down the corridor towards his office. "Look, Al," he stated. "I'll have you transferred to juvenile division in a couple of weeks. In the meantime you had better start getting yourself a working plan and a board of directors together."

As I walked out of City Hall that day I was completely exhausted. I felt like a track star who had jumped several very high hurdles. The only difference was that I knew I had invisible help pushing me forward and lifting me over each new obstacle.

CHAPTER IV

My work in the fifth precinct would soon be finished, and I hoped I could conclude these last two weeks with a bang. From the beginning I had been faced with a choice. The pressures and idiosyncrasies of police work were often difficult to handle. Although I couldn't be a part of all that went on, yet I didn't want to separate myself from the others to the extent that I couldn't get close to anyone. I knew that even though I didn't have much time to spend counseling with citizens, I had plenty of opportunities to talk with other guys on the force. And I wanted to make the most of these opportunities. I wanted these last two weeks to be special. And, they were.

A few weeks earlier we had gotten a new squad car in fifth precinct, so three fellows were chosen to take over the new beat for a while. I was one of the lucky ones. Charlie Besser was another. Charlie had a special reputation down at headquarters. Tall, dark, and exceptionally good looking, he had his choice of girls every night. Charlie wasn't just getting a divorce because of one affair; he had more women hung up on him than a normal guy could handle in a lifetime. The other cops were always teasing him about his surplus energy.

After Charlie and I had been working together for more than a week, one night during roll call, he interrupted the chit-chat with this announcement, "Would you believe it, guys? Palmquist is trying to get me converted." An uneasy chuckle passed from one cop to another. "So, I'm going to get him 'laid.' "

The silence was embarrassing. Most of the fellows knew what I stood for, and they also knew that I was happily married. But then a lot of them had been happily married themselves when they first joined the police department. However, it hadn't taken long before they succumbed to one or more of the precarious temptations that confront cops. There wasn't a man in the room that had never been pro-positioned, and there were only a few present whom I hadn't heard boast about their escapades at one time or another.

Finally Sergeant Erickson broke the silence. "Preacher, if you can convert Charlie, you can convert the devil."

I had been witnessing to Charlie and although he listened, each time he'd either argue, justify his actions, or just try to laugh off what I had said. I was beginning to understand what Erickson meant about Charlie and the devil. Although the contest between Charlie and I was supposed to be a joke, I had an eerie feeling that there was another battle about to be fought. And I knew from experience that the devil doesn't joke around.

The following Sunday afternoon Charlie was off duty, so a crotchety old fellow was assigned to ride the squad car with me. His dumpy appearance and crusty personality had "graced" the force for nearly twenty years. I didn't know if he was just worn out and ready to retire or what, but he definitely wasn't the dashing image of law enforcement.

As the afternoon wore on, we were called to answer a complaint about a loud party. The chance to get a breath of fresh air after sitting in the hot car for hours was inviting. The aesthetic qualities of this partner could have been used for any deodorant advertisement.

When we arrived at the address, the air was vibrating with the loud beat of bongos and electric guitars. Quickly we entered the apartment building and knocked on the door. When the door opened we were greeted by cat-calls from about ten collegiate-type couples clinging to each other and drowning in booze.

While my partner remained in the hall, just staring, I walked across the room and snapped off the stereo. Turning around, I was confronted by a sharp-looking five-foot-five, pretty little blond.

"Is your name Palmquist?" she asked with a syrupy Swedish accent, meanwhile giving a quick tug at my name pin. "I bet you're Swedish too," she continued. By this time she had grabbed my cap and begun to snuggle close to me, running her hands up and down the back of my neck.

The others continued drinking and carousing boisterously, paying little or no attention to me as I tried to silence them. I was wishing that my partner would come to rescue me, but he just continued to stand in the hall with a rather amused, yet dumb look on his face.

Frustrated and embarrassed, I was next to immobilized as this sexy blond continued to rub against me, suggesting that I stay a while or come back after work. Finally I pushed her away from me forcibly and ran for the door, trying to shut out the sound of scornful laughter. I had been propositioned before, but this was the first time a girl had physically tried to seduce me. About then I began to wonder if Charlie did have any connections with the devil.

Back in the squad car I tried to control my anger as I watched my "faithful" cop friend drive along, hunched over the wheel. Eventually I cooled off enough to attempt some conversation. "Why didn't you come in and do something?" I asked, trying to sound nonchalant.

"Nobody ever gave me that much attention!" he replied, almost resentfully. Surprised, I didn't know whether to laugh or feel sorry for the old coot.

Finally, half serious and half joking I retorted, "Well, that's what you get for being a sloppy old crow."

We talked about the situation for a while longer, and, although he wasn't a swinger, he fully expected me to go back after work and take up where she had left off. I tried to explain why I couldn't go back there even though I might have found her desirable, but he just couldn't comprehend. He had heard all that stuff about being a Christian before, but what did that have to do with having a little fun?

The next day Charlie was on the job. Towards evening he suggested that we go see if Milly needed any further help. Several weeks earlier we had been asked to check on a hit-and-run accident. A car proceeding south on Chicago Avenue had hit a parked car, throwing it from the street into the yard.

When we originally went to the door, we were greeted by a beautiful, tall red-head, dressed in a nurse's uniform. I introduced myself and began to fill out the information report for the hit-and-run records. Milly was a divorcee with three children. Her home was as neat as a pin even though she worked full time at a neighboring hospital. The fact that she was not on welfare and also had a Bible lying on the coffee table really impressed me. This gal was not only capable, but she had a few principles besides.

"Look, Milly," I had asked. "Do you know how to collect on the insurance, etc.? If you don't we can get in contact with your agent for you. We'll also try to find this guy who's responsible for the damage."

She was really grateful and assured us that she was completely ignorant about these matters, so we proceeded to search for the driver of the hit-and-run vehicle. A couple days later we found the guy. He had been in trouble with the law a few times before for reckless driving, so he was more than glad to pay for damages in order to avoid further trouble.

Now, a couple of weeks later, we decided to see if she had collected on the insurance yet or needed any further help. It didn't take us more than five minutes to find out that the case had been wrapped up. As we were saying good-bye, Charlie thought he heard the dispatcher calling us on the squad radio, so he left me and ran back to the car.

I was about to follow when Milly reached out and grabbed my arm. "Wait, Al," she whispered. "Stay with me. I love you."

For a moment I couldn't believe what I was hearing. Milly had seemed so stable. She was doing a great job with her family, and I was sure that she had principles. After all, she did have a Bible lying on the coffee table. That was one of the reasons I had offered to give her some extra help.

Now I was flustered. "Milly," I stammered. "I'm married!"

"Does that matter?" she asked, looking hurt and somewhat amazed. "Come back after work. I need you, Al."

I decided I had better appeal to her morals. "Look, I'm a Christian," I continued. "Even though you're a beautiful woman, I couldn't do something like that. I love my wife and I don't think you're that type of woman anyway."

"I'm not going to take you away from your wife," she retorted indignantly. "I just want to spend some time with you."

Unable to get through to her, I just had to turn and run. Little did I realize at that time that I was going to be pursued for quite a while. Several months later, after being tracked from one place to another, I was finally able to convince Milly that I was taken.

The rest of that night I wondered about this new "charisma" which seemed to follow me around. I thought back to the time in police academy when Captain Waller, a twenty-year veteran and a Christian, had taken a special interest in me. His church had supported Teen Challenge in New York; so when he found out that I had worked there, he felt he should advise me how to stay on the "straight and narrow" path while on the police force. He had previously counseled many cops with broken marriages and alcohol problems; so his warning was based on facts.

"Palmquist," he had said, "be very careful. Booze, money, and women are the downfall of policemen."

I could easily understand how booze could block out the depression involved in dealing with destitute people every day. And, money would certainly be a means of compensating for all the frustration that accompanies the inability to change these people and their circumstances, but I couldn't quite figure out why women were such a problem—especially if a cop were happily married.

Now I was beginning to understand. Most women, especially unattached ones, seemed to be impressed by the sharp uniform and the image of masculinity projected by most cops. I guess that most guys pick this up in police academy, and even to me it had seemed that any rookie that made it through police academy had a right to act a little tough. Each trainee was put through a battery of physical fitness tests and was expected to complete them with a score of seventy percent or above in every area.

While I was in training, we had a special course in karate. Our teacher was an ex-marine who felt his job was to weed out the "babies."

The first night he drove us so hard during calisthenics that guys were fainting all over the room. As each fellow dropped to the floor, a sickening smile spread across his face. I was feeling rather dizzy and would have fainted myself in a few seconds if he hadn't stopped.

This took place three times a week for sixteen weeks. So, those of us who finished figured we were man enough. I wasn't completely comfortable with this accomplishment, however. Deep down inside I realized that in trying to meet the world's requirements, e.g., seeking to fit the "cop" image, I had also begun to think like the world, to evaluate situations like any other guy would. I had become self-confident and proud too. But right from the beginning God had a way of showing His contempt for my attitude.

One night three of our instructors who had black belts in karate were horsing around in front of the rookies. As they attacked each other, one of the guys made a clumsy move. "Man, you're nothing," I laughed jokingly.

Turning around, he stared coldly and asked, "Who said that?" The silence was heavy. One by one fingers started pointing at me.

"Palmquist, get out here on the floor. I'll show you who's nothing!" he snapped.

Baiting me as a lion baits a lamb, he let go with several karate kicks to my leg. He kicked so fast I couldn't see his leg a couple of times.

"Go get him, Palmquist," the others cheered. "You can do it. If nothing else works, hit him with your Bible."

I outweighed him by forty pounds and had been practicing diligently; so, gathering all my nerve, I squared off in karate position. Spinning around, I quickly gave him a front kick which connected in the stomach, causing him to fall backwards. While he tried to catch his breath, I threw a couple punches and a chop to the back of the neck, followed by a side kick.

By this time the guys were standing up cheering. That's when it all happened. Before I knew it, he had punched me in the chest. Then grabbing my belt he started twirling me around the room. I felt like a piece of spaghetti being wound on a fork.

Finally, he let me go with a thump on the floor. Grinning from ear to ear, he walked over to me, stuck out his hand and helped me to my feet. Then, facing the class, he asked, "O.K., who's next?"

I obviously didn't have any charisma that time, and, as I quit reminiscing, I decided I didn't want any now. Feeling rather depressed and confused, I began to think about what Jesus had said to His disciples. "One who has bathed all over need only his feet washed to be entirely clean." As I went home that night, I was awfully thankful God had put that verse in the Bible. I couldn't help but be contaminated as I lived and worked in this job. But, I praised God that He had made a provision for me to get clean daily.

The next few days were routine and passed quickly. I had worked in fifth precinct for three years. In a few more hours I would be officially done in this precinct and beginning my career in the juvenile division.

With only a few more hours to go, it seemed that I needed one final reminder of what lay ahead. Charlie and I were patrolling when we were called to an apartment house on 29th and Bryant. Some gal had come home from work and found her roommate unconscious from an overdose of drugs.

Rushing to the scene, we found the girl lying on the bed, unconscious, not breathing, and stark naked. The roommate had panicked to such a degree that she hadn't even thought to throw a blanket over the girl.

As Charlie called an ambulance, I began mouth-to-mouth resuscitation. In a few minutes she began to struggle. Finally she gasped, turned onto her side and vomited. As we sent her off in the ambulance that night, I didn't feel quite as helpless as I usually did when confronted with hopeless drug addicts. Starting tomorrow I was going to be able to do something about them.

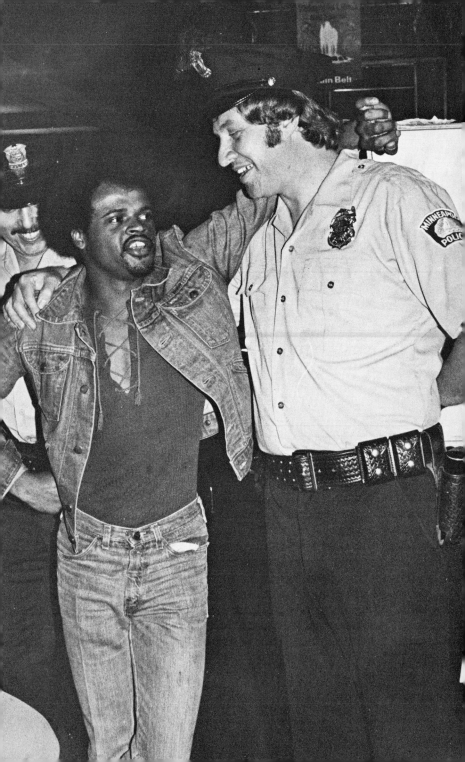

CHAPTER V

The next day I was down at City Hall by 8 a.m. sharp. I had heard rumors in the past couple of weeks that some of the guys in the juvenile division were opposed to my coming into the department, but I really didn't expect any outright opposition. I guess I thought it was such a great program and idea that everyone would be overjoyed.

Inside roll call room a few guys were standing around chewing the fat. As I entered, one of the fellows turned and asked me what I was going to be doing in juvenile division. As I told him about my intentions and hopes concerning a drug rehabilitation program, another guy edged close and interrupted.

"I didn't know drug rehabilitation had anything to do with police work," he commented. His facial expression tightened as he continued. "A policeman's job is to make arrests, not to rehabilitate."

By this time the whole room had gathered around, half expecting a little fireworks. I didn't stop to evaluate the pros and cons of getting involved in a discussion at that moment. I just gave them all the logic I could think of.

"What's the difference?" I asked. "Aren't we all concerned that people quit getting arrested?" I could hear one or two guys clearing their throats as I paused. "All those junkies you've arrested get out of jail and back to the street right away, don't they? However, if we can get a drug addict involved with Jesus Christ, his chances of being arrested again are next to nil."

I was beginning to make an advance in the ranks and felt like pressing the issue but didn't want to start my first day in juvenile late.

"O.K., you guys," I said, chuckling nervously as I headed for the door. "Wait and see."

I spent that first day in juvenile division being orientated to the department. Juvenile division is an investigative branch of the police department involved only with juvenile offenders; so, although my goal was to be released for the drug program, I still had to learn a completely new routine first.

While working on the beat, my duty had been to make arrests and write out the offense reports, but now I was to be a juvenile officer. I would receive reports from other cops and then gather enough material and facts to build a case in court. However, if the kid pleaded guilty to the charges, I didn't have to appear in court but simply hand the report over to the county attorney.

After lunch that day I went upstairs to the planning and research department. Jim Robertson handed me an extra copy of a government form regularly used to apply for grants and told me to get busy. The mayor wanted a detailed report of my goals and objectives along with the proposed methods

50

of attaining these objectives. And, by answering the questions on this form, I was bound to say just about all the mayor wanted to know.

I sat down at a desk in the corner of the room and began to type. First of all I wanted to make it clear that this program would not stop at getting a person free from drugs. We would also be concerned with helping an addict reenter society successfully. There would be no attempt to determine numerically how many junkies could be attracted to the program. Priority would be placed on how many could reenter the community successfully and begin a new and meaningful life-style. I figured we would tackle this goal in three ways: personal instruction, therapy, and vocational guidance.

Selected teachers—probably ministers—would be solicited and encouraged to discuss each personal problem and provide instruction for the program participants. Personal and group therapy would also be utilized. Ex-addicts can help a junkie find himself, and more important, accept himself as a person who can contribute and have a role in the community.

I planned on implementing a vocational program as soon as I could find individuals willing and capable to help in this area. We had to find some way for a junkie to relate to the outside world in which he would have to return to and work as a stable citizen. To help him make the adjustment more easily, we would assign various tasks to him daily. As he progressed, the close supervision would subside.

As I continued I realized that this program would be modeled almost entirely after Teen Challenge in New York City except for one major difference. I wanted this program to eventually be self-supporting, but that would involve owning a business—something I definitely didn't have.

By the time I got most of these ideas typed up, I could see that the future was going to be exciting. Besides a board of directors and a heap of money, I only needed a large house or two and a going business!

For two weeks I had been thanking God for a hypothetical program. It was all so great because God was doing it; but I had never stopped long enough to realize what was actually involved in developing a rehabilitation program from the bottom up. What if it didn't materialize? What if the churches weren't interested? This idea might have too much of a political flavor for them.

The thought of all the faith and patience I'd have to dig up in the next few months was a bit overwhelming. In fact, I was beginning to feel inadequate, so I decided to quit and go home for the day. I knew from experience that there was no use in comparing myself and my abilities with the job ahead. I'd have fun teasing Gayle when I got home. I wouldn't have to wear a uniform now that I was a plainclothesman. I decided that would be good reason to go out and buy a few new "plain" clothes.

The next day one of the narcotics detectives approached me as I walked down the hall. "Hey, Palmquist," he called, catching up with me from behind. "I heard you're going to get drug addicts saved. Don't you know you can't do anything for drug addicts? I think you're crazy!" he snapped.

The Bible says "a soft answer turneth away wrath," but I didn't even have time to think of a soft answer. He just said his piece and strode off down the hall.

That afternoon Robertson called me on the telephone. Three minutes later I was standing in the chief's office, being introduced to a three-member committee from the Greater Minneapolis Association of Evangelicals. They had come to Chief Johnson offering to provide a chaplaincy program which would handle domestic problems, death notices, suicide attempts, alcohol and drug abuse problems, and any other details beneficial to the police department.

They were not only offering a service provision for counseling, but also said they would provide their own car, radio, or other necessary equipment.

One chaplain would be on duty for a twenty-four hour period with a back-up chaplain on call in case of emergencies. The chaplain would respond to a situation only if requested by officers at the scene and would be responsible to the officer in charge.

This was more than the usual offers or suggestions made to aid government. They didn't expect anything in return for their services—only the opportunity to help. It had become apparent to them that the structured church seemed to be missing the boat in urban areas, particularly since so many of the people that were really broken and crushed by sin remained untouched by God's love.

The group of people most aware of these "hurting" people were the police. Yet they had no resources for helping them. For this reason the committee felt that the church should help via the police department.

As I listened to them explain their purpose, I was amazed. It was all so simple. Why hadn't somebody thought of this before? There was nothing special about these three men. It could have been any other pastor with a real desire to love and serve and a willingness to accept the police department's authority over them.

It was obvious that the chief thought it was a pretty good idea and had called me also to find out my reactions. Besides that he probably figured it was a good opportunity to tap their churches for funds and speaking engagements.

As I sat down, the chief turned back to the committee and asked one of the ministers, "How will this work, Mr. Alfors?"

Quint Alfors had pastored St. Louis Park Evangelical Church for twelve years until he became director of the GMAE, an organization interested in starting evangelical programs that individual churches were not equipped to handle on their own.

Dr. Frances Grubbs, another member of the committee and president of the St. Paul Bible College, had been involved in a similar type chaplaincy program in a small Kansas town. Alfors had heard about the idea from him and, investigating it further, felt it would work well in Minneapolis also. The fact that Minneapolis was a large city didn't seem to bother him. And the problems confronted by City Hall were to him the same things that he had dealt with in the pastorate, only several times magnified.

"We know that a lot of police calls involve counseling," he answered. "And we're eager to supply this need, so the officers can keep patrolling their areas. We want to provide spiritual guidance and assistance to people in crisis experiences. We will also try to link them with their own spiritual advisors. However, our ultimate goal will be to introduce people to a satisfying relationship with Jesus Christ. And, I'm sure you'll find this cuts down on crime too."

As I sat there listening I thought about my past experiences working on domestics. Most cops hate domestics and death notices. They feel so inadequate, and I felt the same. Many times I had asked the

Lord to devise a solution to the problem. And now I sensed an answer to prayer unfolding in front of me.

It was obvious that these men were mature spiritually and had a wealth of experience to draw from. Besides this, they weren't trying to present only a historical Christ. He was alive, someone they worked with every day, proving His ability and power.

I couldn't help but remember a few of the domestic calls I had been summoned to. How often I had wished for a chance to sit down with these people and share the answers to life that I had found in Jesus Christ.

About 2 a.m. one morning we were called to a domestic at a lower middle-class home. The husband had come home drunk and begun beating his wife and kids. The noise aroused the neighbors, who called the police.

As we approached the door, we heard moaning and screaming from within; so we didn't wait for someone to answer the door. Inside, the house was in a shambles—curtains torn, chairs overturned, and glass scattered over the floor.

Behind the couch three kids were lying on the floor screaming from pain and terror. Another cowered behind a chair, banged and bruised, while the mother was doubled up on the couch from being kicked in the stomach.

When we first entered, the father was nowhere to be seen. However, as we began giving a little first aid, a big, lumbering brute came staggering out from the kitchen with a sickening grin on his face.

"Boy, I sure showed this family who's boss," he boasted. He obviously expected us to give him an approving pat on the back.

When I had first entered this house I felt like

crying. I began to imagine how miserable a person must be to do such things. I could just picture him tormented by guilt and self-hatred. But, when I actually saw him swagger out of the kitchen, I was gripped by a wave of nausea and a violent urge to lay him out. And, I did. Instead of patting him on the back, I hit him in the face so hard that he landed like a sack of potatoes on the floor.

Immediately I knew I had done the wrong thing. I had thought I could love the unlovely—that is, until I saw him. Then I had taken vengeance into my own hands, but it didn't give me the satisfaction I had expected, nor did it demonstrate Christian compassion—the one thing that was supposed to make me different from other policemen.

Rolling him over, I handcuffed him and asked the wife to make a citizen's arrest, which she gladly did. As I stood there watching her, I was crushed by God's love. "Lord, forgive me," I pleaded. In one quick moment I had even wiped out my chances to tell this woman and her children about Someone who loved them just as they were.

This wasn't the first time that the police had dealt with this family. And there were many more like it. Three to five times a week we were called to help out in family squabbles.

One night we were called to a very wealthy residential neighborhood. The father was more sophisticated in this case. He didn't beat up on the kids; he just destroyed all the valuables in the home. Thousands of dollars worth of valuable paintings had been smashed over the lamps, while several crystal chandeliers lay shattered on the plush carpet.

These two people were rich and well-educated, but by the time we got there to help them solve their argument, they couldn't remember what they were fighting about.

An older officer on the force who had been called to a certain address time and time again often told a story about how he brought this man and wife together. One spring day as he arrived to break up a fight between these people, he got a brilliant idea. Instead of rushing into the house, he first walked around the yard several times until his boots were loaded with mud. Then, entering the house, he scraped his mud-laden shoes all the way across the beautiful rug, smiling innocently as he spread a trail of sticky goo.

When the man and woman who were fighting realized what this cop was doing, they got so upset and angry with him that they forgot about fighting with each other. Joining forces they turned their anger on the cop who simply walked out to the squad car and left. The cops were never called back to that place again.

Once in a while a wife will demand that you arrest her husband. Unfortunately that happened to me when I was riding the squad car with a partner who was only five feet eight inches tall and very skinny. Even though I am six feet three inches myself, I looked like a midget next to the husband we were supposed to arrest. But that didn't make any difference to the woman. She wanted the man arrested and on the double.

I knew I couldn't take him with such a little partner to work with, so I began telling her how handsome and lovable her husband was. In a roundabout way I was telling her I wasn't able to arrest her husband, let alone get him down to the jail. It would have taken half the city to arrest him, but I didn't want her to know that.

Before I had finished, they were trying to patch up their difficulties with a kiss. I got out of there as quickly as possible.

Afterwards I was plagued by despair—knowing that I had conned them until the next time, without actually helping them.

Now, as I saw the committee stand up and excuse themselves, I sighed with relief. God had supplied help in a way that I could never have dreamed of.

As the men left, Chief Johnson turned to me. "Well, Palmquist," he asked inquisitively, "what do you think of this idea?"

"Yeah! I really dig it," I answered. I don't know if my enthusiasm had anything to do with it or not, but his reply was slightly jolting to my equilibrium.

"O.K., that's fine," he stated. "You train them!"

By the time I walked out of the office, my exuberance had declined just slightly. I was thrilled that God was answering my prayers, but I didn't remember specifying that He make use of me in each answer. Now I had two jobs to do and they both loomed pretty big in front of me. Just to be safe, I figured I had better review my prayer requests from the last year to make sure there weren't any more surprises waiting for me.

Mr. Alfors and the other men were waiting for the elevator when I came out of the office. Thanksgiving Day was only a few days away, and I didn't know when I'd have time or an opportunity to get in contact with these men for quite a while so I hurried to catch up with them. The whole time that I had been sitting in the office listening to them, I felt that this was an opportunity to introduce the drug program idea to these men and their churches. I was sure that they could provide unlimited speaking engagements and a good deal of financial support.

Apparently the chief had been thinking the same thing, but because I didn't take advantage of the situation while in the office, he later asked Jim Robertson if he thought I was too timid to head up the drug program. I'm sure the ministers didn't think I was timid as we rode down in the elevator together. I said more on that short ride than I could ever remember saying before in so short a time, and I never was considered exactly shy or reticent.

After I had concluded, I left with a sense of accomplishment and a future date for lunch with Quint Alfors. No one had committed his church for a meeting or financial support, but I could tell that they were thinking about it.

I looked forward to Thanksgiving Day that year. Gayle had invited my parents to spend the day with us. My dad was a retired postal man, and I was eager to tell him about the program and my involvement.

Dad had committed his life to Christ the same week that I had. After going forward at a Billy Graham meeting at the fairgrounds, I went to visit my father who was in the hospital recovering from a heart attack. I told him what had happened to me, and a couple of days later when a nurse tuned in the crusade on his television set, he decided that he also needed a Savior.

Now, after a luscious turkey dinner, he sat in our living room listening to the details of the proposed rehabilitation center. He was thrilled with the possibility of donating his time to help with mailing lists, etc., and little did I know at the time what a blessing he would be to the future ex-junkies.

My Irish mother was satisfied just to know that I would still be a cop. Her grandfather and brother had both been cops, so she had been very pleased when I decided to carry on the tradition. The only reason my mother gave up so soon on my being a priest was the fact that I was "dating" girls when I was in third grade. I guess she figured the struggle would be too long and involved.

CHAPTER VI

I was bored for the first couple of weeks in juvenile division. After working the beat each day for several years and seeing action regularly, paper work was rather dull. I was assigned to work with an older fellow who had been a detective on the force for a long time. But it wasn't more than a few days before he had shown me everything about the department, so we started talking about Midwest Challenge. That was the name I had tentatively chosen for the drug program. This fellow let me know that he was a Christian too; so we had a great time talking about the Lord and the time I had spent with addicts in New York City. He was excited about the possibilities of a similar program here and spent a lot of time advising and encouraging me.

Each day during roll call we were briefed on any available information pertinent to the cases already assigned. However, if we weren't investigating a specific case, we spent the shift patrolling our designated districts. Certain hangouts had a reputation for trouble, so we tried to case these joints regularly, hoping to be a step ahead. If a robbery or burglary took place while we were in the area, we responded as a regular policeman would. The fact that we rode in unmarked cars and wore civilian clothes was often an asset at times like this.

During one of our quiet days I was riding around in an unmarked car when I heard over the radio the dispatcher discussing a chase with another squad car. A green Mercury Monterey had run a red light just as a squad car rounded the corner a block away. When the officer turned on the light and siren, the Mercury sped off, so the policeman gave chase. I was nearby and wanted a little excitement myself, so I headed for the chase.

We finally cornered the car in an alley. The two men in the front seat got out and started running. While the other officers took after the men, I stayed behind with the third party involved, a woman.

As I approached the car she quickly got out and started walking towards me. "Why were you chasing us?" she asked quite innocently. "We didn't do anything wrong."

As she stood there obviously nervous about something, I sensed an inner impression to look in the back seat of the car.

Inside, covering the entire back seat of this handsome Mercury was approximately one hundred seventy-eight dollars worth of fresh, moist, bloody meat. Not satisfied, I started digging around until I found a trench coat with a large booster pocket sewn into the lining. That was all the proof I needed.

In a few minutes the other officers had caught the two men and were on their way back to the car somewhat bewildered. "I sure don't know what we're going to book these guys for," said one of them approaching the car.

"Come on. I'll show you," I told them, pointing to the back seat of the Mercury Monterey. "They've done a little 'extra' shopping today."

A few days later I got a report that a drugstore had been robbed. Two teen-agers were suspect, but I took the mug books along anyway to see if the pharmacist could make any identifications. I also wanted to talk to the people involved to see if I could put the puzzle together.

Driving down the street, I noticed a big moving van proceeding very slowly. In a second, I had another one of those hunches. So I hid in an alley and watched the van go around the block a couple of times. For some reason it just didn't look right.

If most people see a man walking down the street with a ladder at noon, they think he's a painter. I'd think he's a burglar. Cops are trained to be suspicious, and there was undoubtedly something strange about this situation.

Pulling out of the alley, I began following the van. The driver was obviously suspicious and decided to lose me; so I called for another squad car. Within ten minutes we had the three guys in the cab under arrest. The trailer of the van was filled with stolen stereo equipment.

Later that week I had my first lunch date with Quint Alfors. Quint called one morning and asked me if we couldn't meet at some restaurant about 12:30 p.m., so I suggested we meet at the Rainbow Cafe on Hennepin and Lake. I had eaten there often while working in the fifth precinct and knew it was a good businessman's hangout. The homemade vegetable soup was chuck full of goodies—a meal in itself. And, the egg salad sandwiches were delicious. Besides that, parking was free.

As I entered the cafe, Alfors was already waiting

for me in a sunny booth next to the bay window. I wasn't too sure what he expected of me or what his reasons for meeting me were, but it didn't take long to find out.

Quint is a straightforward type of fellow, and he let me know that he intended to give me a thorough workover. There are plenty of "one-horse" operations within the Christian church and, because of this, he was suspicious of a new program starting up. He also wanted to know what my personal opinions and convictions were.

Did I really have firsthand experience with and knowledge of this God I was talking about or was I a good-hearted liberal trying to develop another social reform program? And did I have any administrative ability or that certain touch of charisma needed to direct a program like this? Besides getting answers to these questions for himself, he was asking on behalf of various churches in the Minneapolis area.

The mayor had recently sent a letter to all churches stating that drug abuse was a growing area of concern in Minneapolis and being convinced that the only answer to this was a program similar to Teen Challenge in New York City, he was releasing Al Palmquist, a member of the police department, to start this work. Because of this, he wanted to enlist the help of all churches by asking them to set up speaking engagements for me. However, the churches wanted to be sure they knew what they were getting into before they committed themselves.

Apparently I made a good impression during that first luncheon date with Quint because it wasn't long before he began suggesting prominent members of various churches who could serve on the board of directors for Midwest Challenge.

Jim Robertson also suggested several people for

the board. Eventually we ended up with a twelve-member board. Rev. Gordon K. Peterson, pastor of Soul's Harbor Church in downtown Minneapolis, was one of them. The first time I met him I felt as if I had found a long-lost cousin. His friendly reception and enthusiasm were very encouraging. He immediately invited me to participate in four radio programs on which he interviewed me about the proposed Midwest Challenge and also gave me the opportunity to give my testimony. Later on, I appeared on two television programs for Soul's Harbor.

As a result, meetings in various churches began to trickle in. The first one was a watch night service at Wade Park Wesleyan Church. Although December was rather insignificant as far as progress is concerned, it seemed to pass quickly, leaving Christmas behind before I had time to enjoy it.

Somehow, because it was New Year's Eve, I didn't expect to see many people at this meeting, so the genuine interest was surprising. During the coffee hour that followed I could feel a surge of excitement as the members of the church shot questions at me. The excitement didn't stop with the meeting, however.

I had brought Gayle along that night and, as we headed home, I happened to turn on the radio in the squad car I was driving. About two blocks away another officer was chasing a stolen car. Without a second thought, switching on the red light, I headed for the stolen car to help cut him off. The only trouble was that the light wouldn't work. I was saying a prayer as I sped along, hoping everyone would know what I was doing and watch out for me.

The light and siren aren't used just to scare an offender but are also a means of protection for policemen, especially when there's a chase. It would be so easy for another car to accidentally run into a policeman driving at high speed or running red lights.

As I turned onto another block, I saw the stolen car coming toward me at about fifty miles an hour. Suddenly remembering that I had Gayle with me, I wondered what I should do. Had I been alone I would have turned the squad car across the road to block him off, but now that seemed exceedingly dangerous. Fortunately, I didn't have to decide. A second later the stolen car crashed into a parked car about a half a block in front of us. Later searching the car, we found it full of burglary tools.

No sooner had we started for home again when an accident call came over the air. No one was closer than our squad car, so I answered that call too. In the middle of the street sat a crumpled car, while a hundred yards away another car was wrapped around a tree.

Within seconds an ambulance arrived, so I was free to leave. Returning to the car, I found Gayle looking somewhat pale. "I think that's enough excitement for this year," she said, almost moaning.

During the next week the Minneapolis *Star* and *Tribune* ran a short article about the police department being involved in a drug rehabilitation program. Of course, only the most ardent and persistent newspaper reader would ever have found it. It was hidden some place on page seventeen and didn't seem at the time to be worth much.

However, a couple of days later two junkies called up and wanted to know if the program had begun yet. They had been the ardent newspaper readers.

This was a real encouragement, not only to me, but also to Chief Johnson. He had begun to get a little nervous about the whole thing. First of all, he was beginning to have reservations because we were policemen, and he wondered if addicts would be willing to trust us for help.

Secondly, as the chief had confided to Jim Robertson, "Everything is going so fast I feel like a pawn on a chess board. I don't seem to have any control over what's happening."

January 2 I was invited to give my testimony and speak about the center at a Nicky Cruz Rally at Soul's Harbor. Nicky was the Puerto Rican teenager who lived among the gangs of New York City. Swinging a baseball bat and carrying a garbage can cover, he had led his gang into many dangerous battles until he knelt with Dave Wilkerson and committed his life to Jesus Christ.

His life was dramatically changed and enriched from that time on. After finishing Bible school, he returned to Teen Challenge in New York to help other gang members and addicts find this new experience. A few years later he felt the Lord wanted him to work with young children, so he began a work of his own.

I used to see Nicky often when he was in New York to visit the center, so I was looking forward to seeing him again. Although I was dressed in full uniform, Nicky remembered me right away. When I told him how the police department was involved in this project, it was almost as if he had a flashback.

Nicky didn't believe that the police could be trusted for such a program.

I was a little discouraged as I stepped up to speak that night. I sensed that Nicky felt it just wouldn't work. However, I didn't know that there was a junkie sitting in the audience until after the meeting when a blond, blue-eyed, good-looking kid approached me and asked, "Hey, can I talk with you? I suppose you can see I've tried plenty of programs but still haven't gotten off."

He was in his early twenties and obviously strung out from mainlining heroin.

"I need help," he continued, "and, I liked what Nicky talked about."

I was upset because we didn't have the program in operation yet, but I tried to establish a person-to-person relationship with him. I explained God's plan of salvation and assured him of the deliverance possible through the Holy Spirit. Then I gave him my telephone number and committed him to the Lord.

Before he left I told him to get involved in an active Christian church in order to occupy his mind and keep himself off the street. I felt rather uneasy about turning him loose like that, since I had never met anyone before who had gotten off drugs alone. A month later, however, I saw him at a Christian coffee house. He had turned his life over to Christ completely and was busily involved in an evangelical church.

Later on in January, Quint Alfors arranged a ministers' meeting through the GMAE and invited Police Chief Gordon Johnson and me to speak. After we had finished, my calendar was booked every Sunday night through the end of May. When the ministers found out that we wanted to glorify Christ through this program, the connection with City Hall didn't bother them much. In fact, they were rather excited about the uniqueness of it all.

By the end of January I had found the house that I considered right for the center. I had been looking for a place ever since I had transferred to the juvenile division, but it hadn't been an easy job.

I had contacted a realtor who was an old friend

of mine back in Bible school days. In fact, John was the one who had convinced Gayle and me to attend Bethany Fellowship Missionary Training Center.

Now after looking at more than two hundred photographs of various houses throughout the city, I began to wonder if maybe I wasn't being a bit too fussy. I wanted something similar to 416 Clinton in Brooklyn. I was especially interested in finding a house that had a room big enough to be used as a chapel. I had so many fond memories of preaching and leading kids to the Lord in the Brooklyn chapel that I hoped to duplicate that action in Minneapolis. So, being that the chapel would be the most important room in the house, I was looking for a place that would be conducive to meditation and prayer while still lending a bright and cheery appearance.

It was a Thursday morning when John called again. I was home in bed with the flu. I felt miserable. I had chills and ached all over.

"Hello, Al?" he asked as I halfway moaned, "Hello," into the receiver. "I think I've found just the place you've been looking for," he continued. "How about meeting me at 3045 Columbus Avenue in an hour?"

There was a long silence. I was trying to decide whether or not this was worth getting out of bed for. I had chased around looking at houses for so long that. . . .

"Hey, Al, What's the matter? You still there?" he asked.

"Yes, I'm here," I groaned. "This had better be a good one," I continued, "'cause I've got the flu. O.K. I'll meet you in an hour."

As we entered the three-story frame house, we were ambushed by a maze of horrible colors. Dark old green wallpaper with wretched pink flowers covered the entryway. On the right was a large room which I could immediately picture as a chapel. Although it was a drab brown color, there were plenty of windows for good lighting. And we would be able to seat at least seventy-five or more people in there for services.

Making our way through the upstairs bedrooms, we were forced to weave in and out among little old ladies lying on messy urine-stained beds. This was supposed to be a rest home for mentally retarded women, but because of new regulations the owner was being forced to sell.

I thought it was a pretty good idea myself. At least the place would have a chance to get aired out.

Nearly choking from the combined stench and chills, my imagination was still able to visualize this place all fixed up and full of problem people.

The owner, a stocky little red-headed Jewish woman, was asking $31,000 for the place completely furnished; so I made an offer of $24,000. I knew I was sticking my neck out offering that much, but I felt that this was the place God wanted us to have.

The next day we had our first board meeting. After we had elected officers, I proceeded to tell them about the house and the fact that the owner had agreed to sell for $24,000 with a $6,000 down payment. Everyone was excited about it, especially when I added that we had a grand total of $400 in our bank account.

Our treasurer-elect, Harland Erickson, vice president of Northwestern National Bank at Lake and Nicollet, was very kind about the whole thing, however. After taking a few deep breaths, he agreed to stick his neck out also and try to finance this "shaky" deal. He wanted some time to check it out first, though. So I spent the next few days praying that the computers would feel favorable.

CHAPTER VII

When Gordon Johnson, chief of police, suggested that I help train the ministers for the chaplaincy program, he also told me to work along with Captain Lindberg in the police-community relations division. Captain Lindberg, a well-liked, soft-spoken man, was the first captain of the unit. He had pioneered the idea of community relations in Minneapolis and had been very successful in improving the image of the police department in the community.

We discussed possible ways of training these fellows and finally decided it would be most profitable to have a mini-police academy for preachers. The date was set for February 1.

For the last couple of months Quint Alfors had also been working closely with community relations division. He had also been talking with various pastors around town, enlisting their interest and cooperation and soliciting applicants for the program.

In spite of a cold, snowy day, more than twenty fellows from nineteen different denominations turned out for the mini-academy. We met in the sixth precinct house on 26th and Nicollet.

I had expected them to be "kids" fresh out of seminary or Bible school. But I was in for a surprise. These were mature adult and successful men. They ranged in age from twenty-five to fifty-five years old, and almost all of them were married and pastors of progressive churches in Minneapolis or the suburbs.

These men were keen and eager to get involved. The opportunity to be used of God in a unique ministry within the "big city" was an answer to prayer for many of them.

When I walked into the room that night, there was an unnerving quiet. I couldn't figure out at first if they were afraid, overawed by the responsibilities they were assuming, or just extra-eager students who would be hanging onto every word that was said.

Before I arrived they had gone through legal aspects, administrative structure, and their place and responsibilities within the community relations division. My duty was to familiarize them with slang terms and street procedures, both in class and one by one on the street. It was also my responsibility to let the lieutenant know which, if any, of these men would not fit into the program. We weren't trying to imply that a person who was not accepted for this job was not a good pastor. We were just looking for a special breed of preacher—the one who's as "wise as a serpent and yet gentle as a dove." He would have to have the guts and stamina of a cop combined with the patience and love of Christ.

After being introduced to the men by Bob Turnquist, an officer from the department, I began with the most crucial item in my opinion.

"I hope you guys are really right with the Lord," I began. "Because you just might be laying your life on the line pretty soon."

As I paused for effect, one of the men, a six-foot-three-inch bruiser, let out a roaring laugh. I didn't know if this was just a nervous reaction or if he thought I was trying to be funny, but I couldn't have been more serious. I had only recently been to a couple of policemen's funerals, and several times in the past three years my partner and I had been just a couple of mistakes away from being dead ourselves.

My partner, Don, and I had been cruising late one muggy afternoon when the dispatcher told us to check on some kids in our area who were supposedly shooting guns. We presumed that they were just horsing around, but we hurried anyway.

Arriving at the address, Don pulled into the alley. I was riding in the passenger seat, so I jumped out first. Standing in the backyard holding a rifle was a young black teen-ager, about five feet ten inches tall, weighing one hundred eighty pounds. Two other kids were nearby, but they didn't have guns. At first glance I knew that this kid wasn't horsing around. His face was drawn and tight and his mood didn't seem jovial or goofy.

Walking towards him I said, "Give me that rifle, kid. I want to see it." As I said this, I turned around motioning to Don. But no Don! I was alone in the backyard with three unfriendly teen-agers, one of them possessing a rifle! Don was still in the alley. He had been attacked by a vicious German police dog and was busy fighting him off.

Turning around quickly I saw the kid back up to the porch and level off the gun, sighting in on my head.

"Get away from here or I'll shoot you!" he screamed. He was nervously playing with the trigger.

I could feel the adrenalin surging through my bloodstream, and a feeling of tightness in my throat began to increase. I knew I was on the verge of panicking. As I reached for my gun, I remembered a karate move that the instructor had said would work in a pinch. Using this special front kick, I made contact with his elbow, forcing the barrel of the gun up in the air. The gun went off while the kid lost his balance and fell through the glass door behind him.

After handcuffing him and getting him into the squad car, I spent a few minutes leaning on the steering wheel. I was shaking so badly that I had to concentrate on just pulling myself back together again.

Many squad cars had gathered at the scene; some of the officers were helping Don with the dog. It was hard to tell which one of us was the most unnerved by the incident.

When I first joined the police force I used to work extra jobs for additional money. One of these places was a teen-age dance hall named MaGoo's. There were usually four policemen working together at these dances, but this time it was just I and two other older fellows, somewhat out of shape. Our main job was to act as a reminder of law and order, so it didn't seem dangerous to be understaffed.

The dance was almost over with when a couple of long-haired kids started fighting out in the hall. We didn't know what they were fighting about but figured we had better break it up. I headed for one of them while another officer grabbed the other. I was trying to wrestle one of the fellows off the other when I noticed out of the corner of my eye that someone else was running toward me. He was as big as I—and then suddenly bigger as he jumped on my back.

I put the first guy in a head lock, squeezing as hard as I could and at the same time trying to fight the new one off with my left hand. All the while he kept trying to get something out of his side pocket. His pants were awfully tight so he was having some difficulty getting at it. Just as I was beginning to lose ground, a couple of officer friends of mine drove up to say "Hi." As they walked in the door, the kid who had attacked me finally got a long, narrow switchblade out of his pocket. Fortunately the officers reached the kid before the blade reached me.

Another time the dispatcher sent us to answer a regular domestic call at 3rd Avenue and 22nd Street. Pulling up to the curb, we got out and started walking toward the apartment house.

Just as we reached the step a woman came sailing out of the door saying, "Don't go in there! My husband's sitting on the couch determined to shoot a policeman tonight!"

"Wait here," I said motioning to Don. "I'll get the shotgun." Inside the hall I positioned myself behind the half-open door, shotgun in hand.

"We're not going to hurt you!" I yelled in to him. "Just throw the gun out here."

"I know," he answered back, laughing weirdly. "I'm going to hurt you." I talked to him for quite a while longer and was finally able to convince him to throw the gun out into the hall. I wasn't sure, though, if this gun was a decoy or not, so I told him to come out with his hands up. In the meantime, since the man had a gun, my partner had told the dispatcher to send another unit to the scene.

As he made his way toward the door, I handed the shotgun to another officer who had walked up behind me. Diving for the guy, I tackled him, knocking him to the floor. Having rolled him over and handcuffed him, I asked him what he was trying to accomplish.

"Oh, I thought it would be neat to get my name in the papers for shooting a cop," he replied. I could tell by the weird expression on his face that he wasn't joking.

This was only one of many times that I had disarmed someone in Minneapolis. In fact, I had felt much safer when working in Spanish Harlem in New York City.

Another incident occurred about 11 p.m. one night when we were just about ready to quit. Cruising along we saw a '63 Ford coming down Park Avenue weaving from side to side. In an instant Don and I were looking at each other and bemoaning our fate. "Well, it looks as if we won't get home on time tonight," he said, switching on the siren.

We figured he was a drunk driver; so we pulled him to the side of the road at 28th and Park. "I'll handle it," said Don, motioning for me to sit still as he got out of the squad car.

I turned on the top light in the car and began reading the paper. This was the night that Charles Stenvig had won office for mayor of Minneapolis. I didn't know Stenvig at that time, but I was interterested in the election because a policeman was running for office. That's why I had picked up an early edition of the morning paper.

I was thoroughly engrossed with the election returns and stories when like a bolt of lightning a thought flashed across my mind. "Get out of the car. This guy's got a gun." Throwing down my newspaper, I jumped out of the car and walked up to the passenger side of the '63 Ford.

"Get out of the car," I ordered, pointing my gun at him. Meanwhile Don looked at me as if I had lost my senses. I knew he was wondering what I was doing. It just isn't necessary or ethical to pull a gun on a routine traffic stop.

Within seconds the driver of the car had gotten out of the car and laid his stomach across the hood of the car, his arms stretched out in front of him. He obviously knew what position to take without our telling him.

Normally, I would have frisked him, but it seemed as if I had special radar that night. Immediately I reached around his waist and grabbed a gun stuck under his belt. Pulling it out I turned to my partner and said, "I think the Lord told me to do this. If I hadn't obeyed, you could have been dead." A month later this same man shot and killed someone else.

After relating these stories to the ministers, I began familiarizing a more sober group with slang terminology used by the police department. For instance, "Go to McDonald's. There's one to go. That doesn't refer to a hamburger," I said.

"If the dispatcher calls you to assist with a drunk, he will refer to a D.K. When you are told to check on some D.K. who is disturbing the peace, that simply means some drunk is raising a ruckus."

At 3 a.m. one morning I saw a drunk stumbling down the street. It had been a slow, dull shift, so I decided to have a little fun.

"Psst, psst. Hey, man," I whispered into the squad microphone. "This is Saint Peter talking. Your time has come. Are you ready to enter the gates?"

Spinning around, the D.K. began scanning the sky nervously. He was really shot, so I drew his attention to the squad car. As he stumbled over to the car, a sudden twinge of conscience hit me. I had been playing games with someone else's sad state of affairs. I tried to argue with my conscience. After all, I was just relaxing a bit. I couldn't always play it straight or the job would begin to get to me.

Still I had an uneasy feeling. Hadn't Jesus made it possible to suffer with the suffering? And I had treated the guy like a bum. He must have been important to someone though. And, I knew that if my religion was more than theory, he was very important to God—important enough to die for.

Bringing him back to reality, I arrested him and told him he had better mend his ways. I knew that in the beginning he had chosen this road for himself, but now he wasn't able to cope with it. And the church wasn't doing much to help him either; but as a member of the church, I wanted to reach out my arm and encircle him, sharing his grief. However, the only thing I could do was arrest him. At least he would have food and shelter at the workhouse.

Another time we were called to help a D.K. breathe more effectively. Residents at 24th Street and Tenth Avenue South had looked out the window and noticed a pair of violently kicking legs sticking out of a garbage can. Afraid to tackle the problem themselves, they had called the police. When we got there we had to lift the screaming, garbage-smeared drunk out of the can and into the paddy wagon. He had been hungry and while rummaging through the garbage cans had fallen into one head-first. Luckily, he had been able to support himself with his arms or he might have suffocated eventually.

I continued to define various terms used in police code:

P.D.—fender bender; property damage at scene of accident but no one hurt.

P.I.—personal injury.

D.O.A.—dead on arrival.

O.B.—someone having a baby and not making it to the hospital.

I was getting carried away with all my little stories, but the fellows seemed to be enjoying them; so I risked telling them another one that came to mind.

My partner and I had been catching a few nods of sleep over by Lake Harriet when we heard the dispatcher talking to two rookies. Apparently there was an O.B. call and these rookies couldn't find the address; so, being only two blocks away from the address, we decided to answer the call. When we arrived at the house, I was the first one out of the squad car again, so I hurried up three flights of stairs to the apartment. The first flight was regular stairs, but from then on I had to climb a steep, narrow spiral staircase.

The husband was just coming out of the door as I reached the top of the stairs, huffing and puffing. "How far apart are the pains?" I asked trying to appear cool and calm. I had never answered an O.B. call before.

"Pains nothing!" he replied. "The head is coming out!"

All of a sudden I felt faint. A few weeks earlier another squad car had been sent to answer an O.B. call. When the officer told the dispatcher that the pains were five minutes apart, he received this answer, "All the county ambulances are tied up now. You had better wash your hands."

Don and I had laughed hilariously at the time but now it was on our heads. And, to complicate things, everything that I had learned in First Aid class seemed to have vanished.

Don reached the top flight of stairs just as I turned around.

"Oh, boy! We're going to have to deliver a baby," I said, half choking on my own words. I didn't know whether I should be excited about the chance to gain extra experience or give in to my first reaction and run.

"Oh, don't worry about it," Don replied. "I'm from the farm. It's just like delivering a calf."

By this time we heard the woman scream, so we ran into the bedroom where the woman was writhing on the bed. Don walked over to her and told her an ambulance was on the way. I guess he thought that would comfort her.

I prepared to help and before I knew it I was holding a baby in my hands. About the same time the ambulance driver walked in and took over, cutting the cord and bathing the baby. I was never so glad to see anyone in all my life.

The last code term we discussed that night was "domestic." Domestics are nothing more than family arguments and most of them involve alcohol. The daily logs indicate there are more domestic calls than any other type. They are usually very serious and don't get solved very quickly or easily.

However, on occasion a domestic call is funny. I thought of a funny incident that happened to me.

It is usually the neighbors that call the police department for help when there is a domestic battle going on. Some areas of town are noted for handling things their own way though. One of these sections is Northeast Minneapolis.

However, one night a resident of Northeast Minneapolis began to hear things tipping over and furniture breaking in the apartment above his own. It was an older building and when he heard a big crash and saw the results of it, he finally decided he had better call the police. When he contacted the police department, he said, "I have a man who just fell through my ceiling, lying on my kitchen table. I think I might need some help."

After relating these stories, I dismissed class. It was getting late and these men had put in a long, hard day already.

A few days later Captain Lindberg sent out a memo informing all officers that chaplains would be available with Palmquist during February and operating officially as of March 1.

A couple of nights later I started training the men in a "Ride-Along Program." The first one was Quint Alfors. Alfors was fifty-two years old and a graduate of Moody Bible Institute and Wheaton College with a master's degree in Biblical Theology. He had been a pastor for twenty-five years and was excited about starting on a new phase of ministry.

Gayle and I lived near Lake Calhoun at this time, and I was out shoveling snow when Quint came to get me. It was very windy and I had been playing games with the snow, throwing it up in the air and watching it blow away.

I went back into the house first and got my gun belt. Then we set out for the police garage to pick up a squad car. The temperature was 25 degrees below zero so I was hoping for a "hot" night.

We started patrolling in South Minneapolis. The weather was so cold that even the burglars were home—at least I thought so.

When we reached the intersection at Lake and Nicollet, we received a call that the supermarket on 29th and Nicollet, only a block away, had been robbed. Heading for the scene, I told Quint to stay in the car, out of trouble and out of the cold. However, when we got there the burglar had already fled and the owner was outside pointing in the direction that he had gone. After feeding the details to the dispatcher and filling out the incident report, we set off to look for something more interesting. Unfortunately for Quint, the supermarket burglary was the biggest thing that happened all night. I was happy though. It gave me a chance to let him know more about the Midwest Challenge plans and remind him of the fact that we had found a suitable house but still didn't have enough money to make the $6,000 down payment.

I began speaking in churches more frequently in the next two weeks. This, along with the "Ride-Along Program," tied me up most evenings. During the day I was free to work on the drug program, except for one added responsibility. Because of my past experience and the fact that we would be helping addicts in the future, I had been assigned to the school liaison section. Part of the officers in this section were assigned to problems and crimes in designated schools. Others taught criminal justice courses in the schools. I was assigned to work on the high school drug education program. That included calls to speak at civic clubs, P.T.A.'s and high school assemblies.

It was at one of these high school assemblies that I got the biggest shock of my life. When I had first gone to New York City, I expected the worst and I was prepared for it. But I hadn't expected to find what I did in the Minneapolis school system.

At one school I brought Georgene Stewart, a former drug user, along to help me. I had first seen Georgene sitting in the audience while I spoke to the St. Paul Christian Business Men's Association and felt that I should definitely speak to her after the meeting. Georgene had been off drugs for a few months and was needing work desperately but, due to her record, was afraid to apply for interviews. Her mother had encouraged her to come to the meeting, and while I spoke Georgene sensed that God wanted her to work on the staff of Midwest Challenge when it opened up. After the meeting I realized that she had allowed Christ to redirect her life away from drugs and toward His plan for her life, so I hired her that night.

Georgene had started messing around with drugs while she was in high school. She was what is known as a "garbage head." Her specialty was cocaine, but she also used LSD, speed, and whatever else she could get her hands on.

When she was nineteen years old she decided to run away from home, so she joined a commune in California. She would sometimes sleep with eight men in one night, having been well indoctrinated that this was her place as a woman. And since she was searching for love, she figured maybe this was how she could find it. She began to have doubts, though, after she contracted venereal disease several times.

In the meantime her mother had become a Christian herself and kept sending tracts to Georgene. One day, confused and lonely, sitting in a jail cell, she decided to come back to Minneapolis to go straight. In order to do this, she found a good lawyer and beat the drug charges.

She hoped her life would be different now, but as soon as she got back to Minneapolis, she started using drugs again. She just didn't have the power within herself to resist—that is, until she allowed Christ to put His own strength into her. That was the first time she had ever sensed the love that she had been looking for for so long.

As we walked into the school, I told Georgene I would introduce her to the students and then she could give her testimony. I wanted to snoop around a bit.

I wasn't dressed in uniform, so I didn't draw much attention as I walked through the halls. Several bathrooms reaked with the smell of marijuana, while, in an empty classroom, I found some kid undressing his girl friend. I had heard rumors that there was an open study hall at this school where the kids sold drugs, popped pills, and rolled joints. It wasn't difficult to believe.

Walking back to the meeting, I entered the classroom and found Georgene with eight kids lined up against the wall, telling them how they could have the same type of personal relationship with Jesus Christ that she did, and then praying with them.

The teacher was obviously very nervous about the whole thing.

"What are they doing?" she asked.

"Praying," I answered matter-of-factly.

"Well, can they do that?" she continued, her eyes full of amazement.

I told her what I had just found on my little excursion throughout the school. "And, no one seems to care," I added. "What's the difference if they pray?"

"Yeah, I guess I see what you mean," she said.

As I closed the assembly, one of the kids who had just prayed paid me a first in compliments. When I walked up to the front I heard him say to another, "Wow! A Jesus Pig." During his past experiences with, and attitudes toward, policemen, he had learned to use the word "pig." But now that he had met one who preached Christ, he could only combine his vocabulary—a "Jesus Pig."

Leaving the school that afternoon, I realized that since religion had been taken out of schools, the kids naturally try to fill that spiritual vacuum with another sort of supernatural—drugs, alcohol, and the occult.

During a lecture at a private school in one of the suburbs of Minneapolis, a 10th-grade girl kept interrupting me with inappropriate questions about witchcraft. I didn't know if she was just goofing off or what, so I asked Georgene to take her into another room and speak with her. Georgene spent two hours counseling the girl. The girl's boyfriend had sexually assaulted her and she wanted revenge. As a result she got involved with witchcraft so that she could put a hex on him.

This 10th grader had previously made a profession of faith at a religious crusade. She knew that revenge did not coincide with God's ways, so she sought help from the devil. Georgene warned her that Satan would eventually destroy her life, but she couldn't have cared less. She was completely "turned on" to witchcraft because she had seen a bit of the supernatural. Her closing remark was, "I don't want God's love in my life."

CHAPTER VIII

From February through June of 1972, I continued training ministers for the Chaplaincy Corps two nights a week. Although the Chaplaincy Corps was officially available to the Minneapolis Police Department, the Hennepin County Sheriff's Department, and the Hennepin County Medical Examiner's office as of March 1, I continued to train additional applicants.

By June I had trained approximately forty pastors who worked on a rotation basis. One chaplain would be on duty for a twenty-four-hour period with a back-up chaplain on call in case of emergencies.

The acceptance of the Chaplainy Corps by citizens and police officers was immediate. The daily logs averaged three calls a day for the chaplains. Domestics ranked highest in number of calls. A wide variety of other calls followed, ranging from suicide attempts and death notices to counseling drunks. During these first four months the chaplains logged more than 12,000 miles.

I think the police officers themselves were the

happiest about this additional back-up help. The word had just gotten out that officers could call for a chaplain if needed when our number came over the air.

"Squad 556 . . . 556. Proceed to Lake and Dupont. Neighbors are complaining about a heavy domestic."

"Check," I said, picking up the receiver. "556 proceeding to Lake and Dupont on the double."

Putting the receiver back, I turned to John and smiled. "Well, that didn't take long," I said. John Linch, pastor of a Baptist church in Brooklyn Center, was riding with me for the first time. We had met at the Bryant precinct house at about 7:30 p.m. that night and hadn't been cruising more than an hour when the dispatcher contacted us.

"I'll handle this one," I said to John as we reached the address. "That is, unless you'd like to try," I added, looking at him inquisitively. I knew from previous sessions that most of the chaplains preferred to listen and learn the first time around. They were usually so taken up by the fierce emotions involved and the bizarre conditions seen around them that it took a while to adjust.

"Oh, that's all right," he replied quickly. "You can handle it this time."

Inside the house, it looked like a small tornado had just struck. An eighteen-year-old kid sat at the dining room table, his head in his hands. In front of him, scattered across the table were a couple empty tubes of glue, a hanky, and a paper bag.

Papers and broken glass littered the floor, and several lamps had been turned over by flying objects —probably books and ash trays. There were plenty of them lying around.

"What's the problem here?" I began, turning to

the mother who was trying to regain some composure. According to the neighbors the mother had been screaming hysterically, throwing anything at hand at her son who cordially returned the fire.

"You've got to do something with this kid!" she yelled, half pleading, half demanding. "He's a no good bum. I came home and found him here with this stuff," she said, pointing to the glue. "I don't know why he's done this. I've been a good mother to him."

The kid kept sitting at the table, his head bowed. Apparently all the fight had drained out of him, because he didn't try to defend himself or accuse his mother.

"Have you ever thought of trying some type of spiritual help for your problem?" I asked, turning to the kid.

"Yeah," he answered, raising his head slowly to face me. "I've heard a lot about the 'Jesus' movement. Do you think you could find them and get me in contact with them?"

When he said that, the officers who had called us to the scene began laughing boisterously. This was apparently too much for them. They had found the mother and son raving frantically at each other. Now the kid was asking a cop to help him. This was too strange to believe.

"I know of a coffee house run by some Jesus people," I said. "Come on, I'll take you down there now," I added, giving him a tug on the arm.

In a few minutes all three of us were in the squad car heading for the Heavy Waters Coffee House. Looking over at John, I could tell he felt comfortable in the situation; so I asked him to explain God's plan of salvation for the kid.

As John witnessed to the boy sitting in the back seat, the kid kept shaking his head from side to side.

"Man, this really freaks me out," he said, laughing to himself. "I'm in a police car and you keep telling me about Jesus. I can't believe it."

At the coffee house I introduced him to some of the "Jesus people." They spent the night talking to him, and afterwards when I took him home, he was beaming from ear to ear. He had found reality in Jesus Christ, but he still couldn't figure out how cops could help him find God instead of busting him.

I gave him my telephone number that night and suggested that he spend some time at a Christian communal farm where he could study the Bible and get himself together.

After dropping the kid off at his house, John Linch unloaded his excitement. We hadn't been together more than four or five hours on his first night on duty and already on his first call he had the privilege of directing someone towards the only Person who can change habits and hearts—Jesus Christ. No one could have convinced him that the chaplaincy program wouldn't work.

He had already seen it in action. "Think what would happen," he said excitedly, "if this idea spread to cities all over the United States. There's no telling what might happen. We could reach criminals before they harden behind bars. We could counsel families before their mushrooming problems end up in a divorce court. Why there isn't an institution around that would bar its doors to us if we came to them under the authority of government!"

I had to laugh. Such enthusiasm was good to see and I agreed with him, except that I was still feeling a little conflict within myself as to how my role should be worked out. I knew one thing for sure though: God isn't hampered by government or those in authority over us. He does and will use them to fulfill His purposes.

Some of the pastors I trained were from the suburbs and had never seen or experienced the inner city life, especially crime. One night we were called to a domestic in a black, lower economic community. When we reached the home, the pastor and I were greeted by a black family, shouting and screaming hysterically at each other and at us. I was a "honky pig" and the poor chaplain was worse yet.

I was busy trying to keep them away from each other, so I didn't pay much attention to the pastor. When I finally got the people quieted down a little, I told them that I had a minister along who could possibly help them if they would care to talk to him.

Turning around to introduce him, I saw the chaplain leaning against the wall, petrified, perspiring, and very pale. He couldn't say a word!

About the same time, another squad car drove up to see if we were all right. Walking in, they found the minister glued to the wall with a blank look on his face.

"Is this the Chaplaincy Corps?" one of them asked, snickering softly.

"Don't worry," I replied. "After my expert training he'll be O.K." I was trying to kid with the chaplain so he'd relax, but I could see that it was no use. He was too scared, so reluctantly I took over.

Afterwards he seemed to relax a bit, but he just kept repeating, "Wow! I've never seen anything like that before."

There were also a few things on Hennepin Avenue,

downtown, that most of the ministers had never seen. Police are often called to domestics in questionable joints on the avenue. There were two places in particular that were part of the "education" of chaplains. One was a place for normal bad guys; the other was a hangout for abnormal bad guys.

I usually brought the trainees to the normal place first to show them the ropes. It was better for their equilibrium.

One of the fellows I took to this strip joint handled himself well. We had just entered the bar when a bleached blond bomb in sexy tight black clothes headed for the chaplain. I saw her coming first so I ducked around the corner quickly to see how he would handle himself.

"Hi'ya baby," she said in a syrupy voice, all the while posing seductively in front of the chaplain. "How about a drink?"

The chaplain was trying not to be rude but still wanted to avoid looking at her for fear of what he might see. His face was already crimson as he looked frantically around the room for me.

Finally he half squeaked a reply. "No, thank you," he began, "I'm here with the police."

Within seconds she seemed to shrivel up like a hot souffle just hit be a draft of cold air. Spinning around, she disappeared to the darkest corner of the room as quickly as possible.

I couldn't keep a straight face as I came up behind the chaplain and tapped him on the shoulder. Turning around, he sighed heavily with relief as he said, "Thanks, pal. I'll do the same for you sometime."

"Oh, don't bother," I replied laughingly. "The next time I come to speak in your church, I'll let your congregation know how well you handled yourself."

"Don't you dare!" he snapped back jokingly. "I've got to live."

Although he was only teasing, I knew that the experience had been a strain on him. He had handled himself well, but yet I knew there was a conflict within him which is common to many Christians—whether to risk getting your hands dirty and maybe even hurt in an effort to reach those involved in things we consider "bad" sins or to stay clean and pure for the sake of our Christian example and witness.

When I first met the chaplaincy committee in the chief's office, I had wondered if these guys really understood what they were getting into. Could they stand up under the pressures and temptations that accompany an outreach to wanton sinners? Now I could see that most of the ministers that I took down there were super-embarrassed just to be seen in a joint like that, for which I didn't blame them, but nevertheless I encouraged them to get used to it. "You never can tell when you might be called there officially."

After the chaplains adjusted to prostitutes and naked women (which they actually never did) in the normal bad guy places, I took them to a homosexual bar on Hennepin Avenue. And each time they got the show of their lives.

Inside, the bar is shaped like a big horseshoe so that when a person enters he can get a full-blown view of homosexuals kissing and making out all over the place, not to mention anything about what goes on in the booths. Even though I've been called there numerous times, it still bothers me a lot, and many of the ministers actually felt like vomiting.

I was training two of the fellows on St. Patrick's

Day night, so I decided to take them to this bar. As we walked in the door, I noticed that one of the ministers had awkwardly crossed his hands in front of himself.

"What in the world are you doing?" I asked, not being able to believe what was already beginning to dawn on me. "You don't possibly believe they will try to get you, do you?" I asked chuckling.

He just looked at me rather sheepishly and shrugged his shoulders. I guess I had momentarily forgotten just how naive some pastors are, especially those who have led sheltered lives before becoming pastors. At other times I have wished that I could return to that naive state—in fact, I have often wished I could run a spray of water in my ears and through my mind to clean out all the filth I have had to listen to on this job.

While we were standing there a little "green fairy" came up behind me and began making obscene suggestions. He was dressed in a bright green jump suit and a frilly yellow blouse. A perky green hat was cocked to one side of his head. He kept offering to buy me a drink, in the meantime finding excuses to touch me. He looked so ridiculous that I could hardly keep from busting up and he was so small that he didn't present any real danger to me. I tried several times to witness to him about his need, but the music was blaring too loudly. It was no use, so we just turned around and walked out.

Afterwards I did a little explaining to the pastors. The one really didn't understand what it was all about. I explained the difference between homosexuals and lesbians and told them that both groups can be one of the biggest and most dangerous problem makers for cops and society in general. For instance, there is nothing like a bear robbed of her cubs except a lesbian jilted in love. That's why we were so confused one night when we were called to a lesbian domestic at 22nd and Park Avenue. The neighbors had called for help because of all the racket in the apartment. When we entered we found six lesbians and an old wino.

Some of the girls, dressed in masculine clothes and having butch haircuts, were just getting up from the couch when we came in. Another was coming out of the bedroom with the wino, empty bottle in hand. It was apparent that they had all been fighting, but they had quieted down a bit before we got there. Maybe they had sensed trouble coming.

We asked the girls what the wino was doing there, but everyone just acted stupid. We expected trouble with a group of lesbians together, but the wino seemed out of place. Lesbians just don't have any time for men.

While we stood there pondering the situation, another squad car drove up and Sergeant Suek walked in. Suek had been my first supervisor. He was six feet seven inches tall, a virtual bulwark of strength. Any football player would have been proud to have his neck and shoulders. Yet he was one of the most gentle men I have ever known.

Within seconds he had hashed the situation over in his mind and had come up with the answer.

"Let's see your I.D. cards," he said to the girls brusquely. Not one of them was of drinking age, and yet they smelled like a vat full of fermenting grapes. "O.K.," he snapped, turning to the wino. "I know what your game is. You get what you want as long as you supply the booze."

The wino just stood there, looking like the cat who had chewed the canary. The only trouble was that a few of the feathers were still hanging out of his mouth.

He was booked for contributing to the delinquency

of minors and the girls were sent home because they were juveniles!

I had no more than finished relating this story to the two chaplains that I was training when the dispatcher announced that a St. Paul squad car was chasing a stolen car west on Highway 94. We were only a block away from the freeway entrance at the time, so I figured I had better get in the act. There was always the possibility of a shoot-out and we were behind the squad car and the stolen vehicle so I pushed the pedal to the floor. The pastors that had been so naive about the homosexual joint was sitting in the front seat with me, while the other pastor was in the back seat.

There was a lot of traffic that night and cars weren't able to get out of the way easily, so I began weaving in and out of cars and driving on the shoulder in order to get around them. We were cruising at about 100 miles an hour when I heard a strange noise coming from the back seat. I looked into the rear view mirror and saw the reflection of the chaplain, whimpering and cowering like a shriveled up prune.

Meanwhile the other chaplain was sitting in the front seat with a big grin on his face. He was enjoying the chase thoroughly.

By the time I got to the scene, it was all over with, but it proved one thing to me. Some guys can take pressure in one area while others excel in another. The same goes for falling apart.

About the same time as this incident, the Minneapolis *Star* and *Tribune* ran an article by Robert T. Smith on the Chaplaincy Corps. He merely outlined the proposed program and speculated a bit on its possible worth. However, the effects of the article itself were evident a couple of nights later. I was patrolling with Mark Deynes, pastor of the Fridley Assembly of God Church, when a domestic (gun involved) was broadcast.

"Chaplains won't be called to domestics like this because of the gun," I said, turning to Mark. "But I'll take you over for a look, anyway, if you'd like."

"It's O.K. with me. Let's go."

In a few minutes we turned into an alley and pulled up in back of a parking lot at 27th Street and 2nd Avenue.

"Stay here," I said getting out of the car. "I want to find out if they've got the gun first. Then I'll come back and get you."

A hundred yards ahead of me eight policemen had congregated behind a Chevy station wagon. On the ground was a great big guy, several officers on top of him still. As I approached the group, one of the officers managed to disarm and handcuff him. A second later he was on his feet being pushed forward to a waiting squad car.

All of a sudden he looked around him angrily and with a stream of profanity screamed, "I read in last Sunday's newspaper that there was supposed to be a chaplain around to help guys like me! Now where . . . is he? Or is he like the cops—never around when you need them?"

I was beginning to feel a bit strange as each successive policeman turned his head questioningly toward me, so I just pointed to my squad car and yelled.

Mark was really together. He began listening and counseling immediately and within fifteen minutes had this big bruiser purring like a kitten. After praying with him, they went from the parking lot back to the apartment. He had been fighting with his wife and had gotten very upset when she threatened to leave him, taking the kids along with her. As a result he beat her up quite badly. Now he wanted to apologize.

When we left that night the man and woman had both agreed to forgive each other and had promised to get involved again in their own church.

Another time one of the chaplains and I were called to a domestic in a second floor apartment. When we arrived we found that the wife had big lumps all over her head from being beaten up. The husband was apparently one of these guys who gets belligerent when he drinks. We weren't able to determine any other reason for beating up his wife so badly.

We tried to counsel them, but it didn't take long before we realized that it was useless. She didn't feel much like talking because of the pain in her head, and he was too drunk to reason with.

I knew it was too dangerous to let him stay home in his condition, so I tried to explain to him that I was taking him to the detoxification center until he sobered up.

"I'm not going anywhere with you," he answered, cursing loudly at me.

"Look, mister, you can go one of two ways," I replied. "Either you'll be a gentleman and walk to the car, cooperating fully, or I'll have to take you forcibly and handcuff you."

"Listen, you pig," he continued, the hatred oozing out of his eyes. "You're going to have to take me."

As I watched him, my memory turned back a few months to another time when I had to take a drunk to the detoxification center. That time the guy was a little heavier though. He weighed two hundred fifty pounds.

Bending over to lift him into the squad car, I

felt a snap in my back. When I straightened up, my back hurt so much I could hardly walk. I managed to get him down to the jail, however, and through the whole booking procedure—that is up to the last window. Just as I was beginning to relax and was somewhat off guard, he turned around and gave me a sucker punch. I couldn't think of anything else to do but block it with my shoulder and, as I did, he was knocked off balance and hit his head against the wall. Spinning around, he fell directly with the back of his head on the hard concrete floor. It sounded like a coconut being crunched.

The next day I was in bed with a very sore back while the drunk was in the hospital having brain surgery. Needless to say, I didn't stay in bed very long after learning that. I had to get downtown and start writing out reports. I had tried so hard to be a tough cop without being brutal and then innocently something like this had to happen.

Now I wondered about the guy who had just called me a "pig." As he sat stubbornly on the couch, he reminded me a little of the guy who had had brain surgery. He even looked a little bit like him.

Trying to be as gentle as possible, I braced myself and picked him up. As I turned him around to put on the handcuffs, the guy started talking.

"O.K., O.K.," he said, "I'll come. Just let me give my wife the keys for the car and the house first."

Letting him loose, I turned to the chaplain who was with me and began explaining what the detoxification center was. I forgot about the drunk for a couple seconds and immediately paid for my mistake.

Before I knew it the guy had smacked me twice in the mouth and was zeroing in for the third time.

My karate instructor had said that if we tried, we could learn karate so well that we wouldn't think about it—just react. And I had—and did. Two karate punches and one kick later, he was lying in a heap on the floor. As I stared at him lying there in front of me, I kept telling myself there had been no time for a theological discussion on how to best show the love of Christ to this guy while he was trying to knock my brains out—and yet—wasn't there another way? Would this conflict ever be resolved? Or would it remain an occupational hazard as long as I wore a policeman's uniform?

I handcuffed the guy and took him down to the detoxification center only to learn the next day that he was in the hospital with two broken ribs and filing brutality charges. To say the least, I was very frustrated. And I had to spend another day writing out reports. This time I had two witnesses though—the chaplain and the drunk's wife.

Although most drunks get very belligerent, they are often very sensitive and introspective when sober. It all starts when they hit their favorite bar and load up with "3.2 courage." I was riding South Minneapolis one night with one of the chaplains when a request was broadcast for help at a nearby bar. On the way to the bar I decided to tell the chaplain about the first time I was called to a bar fight. An ambulance had also been called to the bar because someone's head was cut. So, since I was driving I automatically threw on the red light and siren. My partner had been on the force for a long time. Leaning over and switching off the siren and light he said, "It's O.K. to use the siren for something legitimate, but this is just a stupid drunk that's fallen off a bar stool."

"But don't you think we should still give it our best?" I had asked. "It might be something different."

"O.K.," he said, turning the switch back on. "Just wait and see though."

I was a bit on edge; so, pulling up to the curb, I rushed into the bar while my partner came dragging behind. The first thing I saw was a guy lying on the floor holding his head. As I bent down to examine him, my partner walked up behind me.

"Would you mind telling my young partner what happened to this guy?" he said, directing his attention to the bartender.

"Sure. This guy and another one were over there having a big argument," replied the bartender, pointing in the direction of the pinball machine. "He was coming back to sit down, missed the stool and fell on the floor."

I was rather embarrassed but at least I could face my own conscience. However, I couldn't get rid of the fact that this was someone I wanted to share Christ's love with, even if only through giving him first aid or helping him to his feet. But my partner didn't see it that way. Putting his arm around me, he laughed loudly. "Stick with me, kid," he said, patting my shoulder. "I know all the answers."

I finished the story just as we arrived at the bar. Four officers were already there. Inside the bar one drunk had another over in the corner, bouncing his head off a pool table.

Grabbing the offender who was playing bounce

ball with the other guy's head, one of the officers said, "Come on, we'll give you a place to sleep tonight."

After setting him on his feet, the policeman let go for a minute and whammo—the drunk was trying to slug the cop. Luckily he was quick enough to just step out of the way, and the drunk went sailing by, self-propelled, head first into the bar.

The officer, who was at least six feet six inches tall, picked him up like a sack of potatoes, laid him on the pool table and handcuffed him.

Later, the bartender tried to make use of his wild imagination by calling the precinct captain and pressing brutality charges against the officer.

We have never had much success in helping drunks because most of them are not willing or able to listen.

However, one evening when the chaplain and I were patrolling around Bryant and 26th, we had a unique experience. We had just started the shift when we spotted a drunk driving recklessly down the road.

Pulling over to the side, we arrested him and put him in the squad car. He didn't resist at all. After ordering a tow for the guy's car, we headed for jail. The chaplain immediately began delving into the guy's alcohol problem.

Within seconds the drunk was telling his story. His wife bugged him too much so he drank to forget. Besides that he had numerous other problems. I have never seen a drunk have instant confidence in a counselor before. There seems to be something so unique about a chaplain working out of the police department that people want to try them out and see if they've got any more answers than the average counselor.

It was a heavy night so we had to wait outside the drunk room. The whole time the chaplain and he talked freely and in-depth. Before it was even this guy's turn to use the breathalizer, they had set up a time for a future appointment.

The rapport between the chaplain and this drunk actually got to be funny. When the officer in charge tried to get the guy to breathe into the breathalizer to measure his blood alcohol content, he couldn't get the guy to stop talking long enough to produce a steady stream of air.

I knew the officer was trying to be polite, not wanting to interfere with the counseling session, but finally he just couldn't wait any longer and had to tell the guy to shut up.

It only lasted for a few minutes, however. All the way up the elevator to the jail he kept expressing his hopes and desires for a new start in life. And after his stay in jail, the counseling sessions continued.

One chaplain had never seen a "high" drug addict, so, when narcotics officers chased a guy who had robbed a suburban drugstore, pursuing him into an apartment, I asked the minister if he would like to see what a junkie looked like.

We arrived at City Hall before the detectives; so, while we waited, I let him know just how short of needed funds we were for the down payment on the house at 3045 Columbus Avenue.

A few minutes later we heard the sound of keys and flashlights clanging as four policemen carried a limp, deadweight mainliner down the hall. He was so high he couldn't possibly have stood on his own two feet. He had robbed the drugstore for drugs but had never even gotten around to using them. If he had he probably would have been dead from an O.D., considering the condition he was still in.

The chaplain and I were standing in front of the jail elevator so, when they approached, I asked one of the officers if he minded my talking to the kid.

"Well, no, Preacher," he answered laughingly. "All we've got to do is to let go and he'll be on his knees already."

Chuckling to myself, I walked into the elevator with the others and turned to the kid. "Hey, have you ever thought of going into a program to get help?" I asked.

"Yeah, I've been every place," he answered like a typical older junkie. You had better get more than human power for me."

By the time he said this, we had reached the jail, so with a face full of despair, he dropped his head against his chest and was carried off. As the door shut on the elevator, I turned around and kicked the side wall forcefully. I was furious! I knew this wasn't a necessary reaction, but the pressures involved in buying a house without money were beginning to get to me. I felt so alone even though other Christians were gradually becoming interested. It all seemed so slow though. What about all the people that would go untouched, unloved before we ever got organized?

"If people don't get this project going and give us some money, I'm going to go out and take it off them physically!" I roared, taking my frustration out on the chaplain.

Another thing that had bothered me was that look of despair on this guy's face. Young drug addicts very seldom seek help because they're enjoying their "highs" too much. But when they start falling apart and can never completely satisfy their cravings, they seek help. This guy was trying to seek, but all he could look forward to was a robbery booking and a stay in jail. And, jail was not the place to find help for drug addiction.

I remembered one of the fellows in New York City saying that the first time he went to jail he was put in a drug program. It consisted of seeing a psychiatrist once a month for one hour. Finally he refused to continue because the psychiatrist was so messed up himself that he couldn't possibly help anyone else.

Reaching ground floor, the chaplain turned to me and asked, "Isn't there anything you can do for people like that?" He had never realized the depth of despair involved in helping "society's corrupters," and he obviously felt helpless. He was also hoping by this question to soothe my frazzled emotions.

"Oh, don't let me bug you," I said more softly. I was beginning to feel a bit embarrassed by my outburst. "We cops see this kind of destitution all the time. The only problem with me is that being a Christian I can't go out and get drunk to erase the memories. I've got to leave them with the Lord and I haven't learned to do this 100% of the time yet.

CHAPTER IX

The first time I met John Owen was at a Greater Minneapolis Association of Evangelicals breakfast meeting. As I finished speaking, this six-foot-four-inch Jolly Joe rushed up to me and enthusiastically began to tell me about his ardent desire to be a police chaplain. He was bigger than I, but still I felt as if I were talking to an excited kid. His effervescent charm unnerved me. I was sure, right from the beginning, that he would never be much more than an ambulance chaser or hobby cop, someone who wants to chase police calls.

My first opinions of John were unfounded, however. As I got to know him better his character and determination made a big impression on me. John graduated from Asbury Seminary with a master's degree in theology and then, with his wife Belva, moved to Minneapolis where he pastored the First Free Methodist Church. It was while pastoring this congregation that he felt that the police department was the perfect mediator between the church and those involved in serious and often destructive trouble.

His first innovation, however, could have been considered a flop. John thought it would be easy to get acquainted with the policemen in the third precinct, only ten blocks from his church, so one night while his wife was working the night shift at Veterans Hospital, he took a chocolate cake and a large thermos of Russian tea and walked up to the precinct house a little after midnight.

After introducing himself through the bars of the locked door, he was admitted and began getting acquainted. Much to his surprise the officers present were cool and rather "stand-offish."

John sat with the men for several hours talking and intermittently offering cake or tea to them. But each time the offer was either evaded or flatly rejected. Finally about 5 a.m., after John had eaten a couple pieces of cake in front of them and was still well, the lieutenant on duty ate the first piece of cake. After that the other men began to eat the cake also. By the time report was over with they were asking him why he hadn't brought more.

Before John left the precinct house early that morning, he found out why the men had been so cautious about the cake. A week earlier a couple of waitresses from a nearby restaurant had brought a lovely chocolate cake to the precinct house. All of the men had indulged freely in this delicious morsel only to find later that it was loaded with Exlax. It was for this reason that John had been an object of suspicion.

John was really anxious to get into the chaplaincy program. He came on loud and strong with a few peculiar mannerisms besides. He just wasn't suitable—I was sure of that; so after my talk at the breakfast where I first met him, I made a quick escape, only to be cornered again in the parking lot. I didn't get loose until I was engaged to speak at his church. He wanted me to start letting him ride with me in the squad car too, but I said I'd call him when I got a schedule set up. We hadn't even had the mini-police academy yet.

When the academy did start, there was John, big as life and full of questions. In fact, John was the one who laughed so boisterously when I told the men they had better be prepared to die. And I don't know if it has been coincidence or not, but John has been in more precarious situations than any other chaplain.

One night when we were short a chaplain I offered to fill in. I was also scheduled to conduct a home Bible study group that same night. Just before the meeting a group of us were standing around oustide the house when a couple of officers that I knew drove by in a squad car. Seeing us there, they stopped to chat for a while.

While we were talking, the dispatcher called about a domestic quarrel at 23rd Street and 12th Avenue South.

"Hey, look, Chaplain," said the officer driving. "We've been there twice already tonight. I think they're harmless. Why don't you go over and take it?"

John was not on duty that night but had come along to the Bible study. So I asked him if he'd mind going since I was supposed to get the meeting started.

Ten minutes later he was entering a shabby home in the middle of the Model City area. Dog and cat manure, mixed with fragments of glass, littered the floor. The officers who had accompanied him there explained the situation to him and left him sitting at the kitchen table, the husband sitting at one end and the wife at the other. A butcher knife was lying on top of the table halfway between them.

John began talking to them trying to find the proper approach while all the while the woman kept interrupting.

"I'm going to kill you," she said, directing her remarks towards her husband.

John made the mistake of underestimating the woman and her remarks. All of a sudden she stood up, turned around and pulled a knife out from the waistband of her slacks. Within seconds a streak of steel was whizzing in front of John's face toward the man's abdomen. Luckily it glanced off the edge of the table, just missing the husband. By this time the husband was heading towards the door, and John had picked up his pack set and begun contacting the dispatcher. Gayle and I were just getting into our car when I heard him screaming, "Help! help! Chaplain 2 needs help!" The only trouble was that he couldn't remember the address.

I knew where he was, though, so I took off for the address. Going down Chicago Avenue at seventy miles an hour, I heard Gayle ask repeatedly, "Why are you going so fast?"

"The chaplain is in trouble," I kept replying, but she didn't seem to understand. I forgot that she didn't know about the situation.

I was the first one to arrive at the home. Running in I found John leaning heavily against a wall. His face was ashen.

After the woman threw the first knife, she grabbed the butcher knife lying on the table and started after her husband. John stepped in front of her, so she turned on him. Suddenly he remembered the address and bellered it into the radio while at the same time using the other hand to knock the knife out of the woman's hand.

It was a few minutes later when I arrived, followed by seven other officers. John was already starting to "disintegrate" when we arrived. The mistake that most people make in circumstances like this is to reflect on what might have happened. That's what John had begun to do when I found him. Already he was pale, dry-mouthed, nauseated, and shaking from head to toe.

The police finally found the husband and wife outside, a little under the weather. "Look, if we ever have to come back to this house again, you're both going to jail!" roared one of the officers who had been there earlier that evening. "We don't have time to play idiotic games."

Another policeman turned to John. "Look, Chaplain, since you don't have a gun, next time grab the antenna of your radio and smack somebody with it."

Although John didn't seem to meet the grade at first, it didn't take me or the other officers long to see that he was serious about this work.

In the process of helping those who called for a chaplain, he also discovered the fact that policemen themselves and their families also had needs that were not being met. The police officer sees so many negative aspects in society that he becomes depressed. People call on him for help and the officer has this image of never needing help himself. But there is a lot of tension and frustration in police work, and sometimes he just needs to unwind with someone he trusts.

However, since their duty hours are irregular

and their work that of a confidential nature, law officers are often forced into a position which does not include a real confidant, either in a co-worker, a family member, or a minister. John, as a legitimate part of police business as well as a trained spiritual leader, felt that he had a maximum opportunity for serving these often-neglected members of our community. And since the corps has met with such a warm response by officers and public alike, when Police Chief Gordon Johnson later asked John to serve along with a Roman Catholic priest as chaplain for policemen and their families, he happily agreed.

The wives of policemen were also happy about having a chaplain. At a monthly luncheon meeting for over one hundred policemen's wives the president of the group said, "I feel as though a great load has been lifted from me. I have been hoping for some time, as have many others here, that the Minneapolis Police Department would provide a chaplain for the benefit of the men, their wives, and their families. I am so grateful to God that He has arranged it."

This new involvement is threefold for John. He serves the Minneapolis Police Department and their families as a pastor in times of death, illness, marital problems, family problems, professional problems, etc. Since many of the families have no active relationship with a church and since much of police work is confidential, John's unique relationship with these men is better than that of a regular pastor.

More specifically, he coordinates the work of the police chaplain corps, supervising the men, working out monthly schedules, assisting with unusual cases, and helping to train in other candidates. This involves a lot of paper work, office management, and correspondence.

Besides this he is trying to develop an effective follow-up program which includes visiting as soon as possible each of the persons contacted by the volunteer pastor, Chaplain 1, during his duty day of twenty-four hours.

Before this visit his "parishioners" receive a letter from the Chaplaincy Corps reminding them of their past contact and encouraging them to make use of the spiritual help available through the corps or their own church or synagogue. Then, while visiting these people later on, John tries to ascertain their openness to having a "Salvation Bible Study" in their home. If they are open, an appointment is made and they have the opportunity of personally committing their lives to Christ.

John then attempts to find an evangelical church in the neighborhood whose members live near the new contacts. The pastor is contacted and brought along to visit the home of those involved in crisis.

The general reception of this auxiliary branch of the police department has been so great that it has even been cited in the Congressional Record by Bill Frenzel, representative from the State of Minnesota. In an article entitled, "Police Get Helping Hand from Clergy," Representative Frenzel quoted this story.

"The Rev. John Owen recently sat across a table in a downtown Minneapolis apartment and listened as a woman in her early forties threatened to take her life with the straight-edge razor she brandished.

"Mr. Owen talked with the woman for seven hours, finally convincing her to seek help. She is alive today and is attempting to cope with her lifelong alcohol problem.

"Minneapolis police say the counseling rendered

by Mr. Owen is responsible for saving the woman's life."

This is just one of many episodes that John has been involved in. One time he arrived too late to counsel an attempted suicide. The man had had a serious drinking problem and made hell on earth for his wife and family. The husband and wife had often fought, but this time, just before he shot himself, the woman had screamed, "I wish you were dead!" And, it wasn't long before he was.

This, of course, left her with a tremendous guilt problem. It was a real privilege for John to tell this distressed woman that God loved her and would forgive her and free her from condemnation. She was offered happiness, peace, freedom and eternal life through Jesus Christ. And, she accepted it—one big package deal. Now she is going through her package, discovering and rediscovering each part and how to make use of it to live successfully in a new life.

Another person that John introduced to Jesus Christ was a sex pervert. He had turned himself in to the police, but since no one had pressed charges, they didn't know what to do with him. Eventually he was referred to the chaplain. He told John his story about numerous trips to counselors and psychiatrists, about group therapy and contemplated suicide, and finally about constant failure while trying to find the answer.

John took this sex pervert into his own home and after a two-hour Bible study, the man gave his life and problems to Jesus Christ.

He is now involved with a church group and is maturing in Christian character. He still finds it difficult, however, to understand why in all his searching no one ever told him about God's ability to love, forgive, heal, and restore.

However, not everyone responds to help. One time John was asked to counsel a man who was not only drunk but high on drugs. He was waving a gun at the policeman, so they suggested that the chaplain be very careful. John was able to convince the fellow to let him into the house, so he went in and talked with him for more than an hour. Eventually the man was willing to put down the gun and be taken to a hospital. Later, however, after being discharged from the hospital, he committed suicide by putting the gun barrel into his mouth and blowing off his head.

Although there are always suicide calls, people seem to be more disposed to commit suicide on holidays. Perhaps they become more aware of their "aloneness" on holidays.

It was a holiday when Sergeant Sanford from squad 110 contacted Chaplain Owen about an attempted suicide. A forty-year-old woman had tried to slash her wrists but hadn't done a very good job of it. She had refused an ambulance and said she would do it right the next time; so the sergeant was concerned about her.

She lived in a seedy third-floor apartment at 15th and Portland Avenue. When John arrived and knocked on the door, she asked who it was.

"It's Chaplain Owen," he answered.

"I don't want to talk to you," she snapped back.

"Oh, that's O.K. May I come in anyway?"

"No!"

"I'd like to talk to *you*," he continued.

A few minutes later the door opened slowly and a tall attractive woman with a bandaged wrist appeared.

"What's your name?" asked John trying to involve her in friendly conversation. She stared at him with a mixed look of hate and pain.

"I don't have a name!" she replied sarcastically.

"Oh, everybody has a name," he said, trying to employ a soothing voice.

"Well, what's yours?" she asked.

"Mine's John. It means a gift of God."

She paused a few seconds, seemingly trying to weigh out the pros and cons of letting him in. Finally, motioning for him to come in she said, "Oh, call me Helen."

"Is that your name?" asked John as he walked past her into the small one-room apartment. The living room had a fold-away wall bed for sleeping, and a small kitchen was set up in an adjacent hallway.

"No, that's not my name," she answered, slamming the door and following him in. "But it doesn't make any difference."

For a while John tried to talk to her, but she wasn't interested and finally got up and walked over to the small kitchen. John got up and followed her to make sure she wasn't looking for something to harm herself with. Next she went into the bathroom with John close behind. After circling back to the living room and fidgeting with her bandaged wrist for a while, she got up again and went into the bathroom. John followed close behind until she spun around and glared at him.

"Will you please leave?" she demanded. "I want to use the bathroom!"

Turning around, he sat down on the delapidated old brown couch and listened as she closed and locked the bathroom door.

A foreboding gloom saturated the room. He felt like breaking down the door, but what if she really were just sitting on the toilet? It would have been very embarrassing.

116

All of a sudden he heard a blood-curdling scream from behind the bathroom door. Even as he rushed to the door he knew what she had done. Unable to open the door, he ran back to his pack set to radio for help.

A second later she had opened the door herself and stood there holding her left wrist while the blood made an arch of eight to ten feet as it gushed from the severed artery. Her left hand dangled, the tendon cut completely through.

In that same instant the apartment door burst open and two cops charged in. One of the men was Sergeant Sanford who had been there earlier. They had been driving nearby and decided to check on things. As they were climbing the stairs they heard her scream.

Immediately one of the officers ran to a hall window, stuck the antenna of his radio out the window and called for an ambulance on siren. Meanwhile Sergeant Sanford grabbed an old rag, clamped it on her wrist and squeezed. His partner returned quickly and found the pressure point.

The whole time "Helen" sat calmly in a chair repeating nonchalantly, "Oh, just give me a cigarette and let me die."

Three to five minutes later the ambulance arrived. Even though she had lost a lot of blood, she insisted on walking down three flights of stairs. She wasn't a particularly muscular woman, but she had plenty of strength to match her height.

John visited "Helen" regularly while she was in the hospital, and finally found out that her real name was Corrine. After a while Corrine was transferred from the hospital to a nursing home for convalescense. During this time John lost track of her.

Then one day when the chaplain was talking to another officer in the property room down at City Hall the dispatcher contacted him, stating that he was to call a certain number.

He returned the call a few minutes later and said, "This is John Owen. Who is calling?"

"Oh, just call me 'Helen,' " was the answer.

Immediately the memory of Corrine flashed across John's mind. "Is this Corrine?" he asked hesitantly.

"Yes." She paused. sighing heavily as if really bugged about something.

"Where are you?" he continued.

"I'm at Nicollet and 21st," she replied. "I've got to see you right away."

Giving his address to the dispatcher, John got into his car and headed for Corrine's apartment. Scenes from her previous suicide attempt flooded his mind as he sped south on Third Avenue.

Arriving at the address Chaplain Owen rang the bell. No one answered. Maybe the bell was out of order, so he knocked loudly on the door. No answer. Finally he heard a soft "Who is it?" from within.

"It's me, Chaplain Owen," he answered anxiously. He didn't know whether she was planning on taking her life again or what.

Inside, the chain lock slid open and there in the semi-darkness stood Corrine, her same full, statuesque figure, robed in a soft pink flowing gown. Her red hair framed a beautiful face that would have done credit to any twenty-year-old woman. No one would have imagined her to be a potential suicide victim.

"Come in," she said turning around and walking over to the edge of the bed where she sat down.

Closing the door, John walked into the room and sat down in a chair next to the bed and pulled it around to face her.

"Well, Corrine," he began. "What's wrong?"

"There are four things I want from you," she stated straightforwardly.

"What are they?"

"We'll take them one at a time," she continued.

Not having a clue what she was up to and feeling a bit uneasy, John leaned forward in his chair and interrupted her saying, "O.K. then, let's take the last one first."

Before he was fully aware of what was going on, she had reached up and grabbed him by the arms, pulling him fully on top of herself and whispered, "Rape me, John."

Trying to push away from her, he looked straight into her eyes. "No Corrine. God loves you and I love you, and even though you are very appealing, I'm not going to sin against God or you or myself or my wife."

"No man has ever refused me!" she lashed out scornfully.

"Well, maybe you've never met a Christian man before, Corrine," he replied. "Jesus Christ is in me and can keep me from giving in to the strongest temptation."

Standing up, John continued, "If you really want help, I can help you, but if not, I'm going."

Before he left he asked her why she had tried to seduce him.

"Well, it wasn't because you're John Owen," she laughed scornfully. "It's because you are a chaplain."

119

CHAPTER X

In mid-March we were still $2,000 short of the $6,000 down payment necessary to get the house signed over to us. Harland Erickson, the treasurer of our newly founded corporation, had set up March 31 for closing the deal. With two weeks and $2,000 to go, I was beginning to wonder if April 1, 1972, would really be April fool's day.

I had one big speaking engagement booked before then with the St. Paul and Minneapolis Full Gospel Business Men's Association, but I wasn't at all sure that they would produce the needed funds.

I had brought Mike Estrada, one of the Puerto Rican fellows I had checked into the Teen Challenge Program in New York, along with me to the meeting. Mike had been a junkie for more than ten years. After finishing the program in Brooklyn, he had gone to the farm in Rehrersburg, Pennsylvania, and then on to the Teen Challenge Bible School in Rhinebeck, New York. Mike was married and had a small son now and was training for the ministry. He was a senior at North Central Bible School in Minneapolis, and I figured he was far enough along to be reliable, so I hired him for the staff of Midwest Challenge.

After Mike gave his testimony to the men, I began to preach. I told them what we were doing at the present and what our proposed plans were, the whole time hoping the Holy Spirit was speaking not only to their hearts, but to their pocketbooks. I told them how much money we needed by Good Friday and mentioned that as they left the room there would be a box for contributions on top of the piano.

After the meeting was over, we were only $300 short. I was surely glad that my public relations man, namely, the Holy Spirit, had done a good job. The remainder of the $300 came to us by March 31 in small gifts of five and ten dollar bills from friends and interested people throughout the area.

At 4:00 p.m. of March 31 I walked into the conference room at the Northwestern National Bank and as a corporation officer signed the papers that gave us possession of 3045 Columbus Avenue.

Harland walked me to the door an hour later. "Well, we've signed it," I said. I tried to be casual and offhand, but my heart was pacing a little faster than usual.

"That's right," chimed in Harland, laughing and punching me playfully in the arm. "We can't turn back now."

As I walked out into the street, I felt a whiff of spring wind teasing my face. There was that fresh smell of spring in the air and I sensed a surge of new life, new beginnings in my spirit. Tomorrow we would open the center for business. I was hoping and praying that this work would be a means of new life to many hundreds or even thousands in the future.

I had begun gathering my staff several months earlier. There were five altogether. Mike Estrada had been the first one, then Georgene Stewart.

Louie Rivera was another former drug addict who, after being "strung out" for seven years, entered the program in New York City. When he joined our staff he was a freshman at a Bible school here in Minneapolis.

Bart Foster and Dick Harden also joined the staff at the beginning. Both of them were Bible school graduates, had worked at Teen Challenge in New York, and also in New Jersey. Both were competent counselors and had a very effective rapport with junkies and delinquent juveniles.

When I first contacted Dick he was working in a warehouse. I wanted him to be assistant director of the program, so I called him on the telephone one morning and asked, "Dick, do you think God wants you to be a warehouse worker the rest of your life? Don't you think it's time to get back into what God has given you a talent for?"

"When do I start?" he asked enthusiastically. A few days later we went to lunch together and began working out the details.

April 1 we all converged on the center. Jim Robertson had donated some extra furniture from his home. He and his wife came along with the truckload of furniture to look over the place.

Pulling up in front of the house with a paddy wagon full of furniture didn't seem strange to us at the time; however, it looked mighty suspicious to all the neighbors who were looking on. The expressions on their faces was indescribable. Perhaps had we realized at the time that these individuals were all pushing drugs, we would have been less dumbfounded when a week later, in the middle of the night, they all moved away without even notifying the landlord. They were obviously very paranoid. Since the police department was starting a drug rehabilitation program here, they were sure it was only a cover-up and that we would soon be raiding their homes.

It could be that God was just cleaning up our neighborhood though, so that those who came into the program would have a fighting chance.

About two in the afternoon the first addict walked up to the door. We were all busy cleaning house when we heard the knock on the door. Since everyone on the staff was either scrubbing floors or arranging rooms, we figured it must be a stranger—hopefully one who wanted help.

As I opened the door I was confronted by someone needing help, but he wasn't a stranger. John was a policeman's son whom I had talked with earlier at the Heavy Waters Coffee House. He had already turned his life over to Christ, but the first thing he said to me as I opened the door was, "I want to come into the program. I can't make it without discipline and spiritual growth."

This is what we had been waiting for—a beginning! "We don't have the program completely set up yet," I told him, holding the door open for him to come in. "Actually, all I can offer you is a Bible in one hand and a paint brush in the other."

He was willing and we were elated.

The next day the problems started, however. I was sitting in my office (a front porch which had been closed off at one end), working over some lesson plans when a young man about twenty years old came to the office door. One look told me he was in trouble. He was extremely nervous and looked as if he were ready to dash out the door at the slightest hint of difficulty. "Are you a cop named Palmquist?" he asked, keeping his distance.

"Yes, I am. Come on in," I replied.

"I heard I can trust you. You won't arrest me, will you?" he continued. His eyes were pleading with me, yet his face was a picture of doubt.

"No, I won't arrest you," I answered. "What's the problem?"

"I think the police want me," he blurted out.

The only trouble was that when I asked him what for, he didn't seem to know. I figured I had better call the Hennepin County Warrant Office and find out what was going on, so I suggested he sit down and relax a bit.

The officer I talked to promptly informed me that there were four warrants out for a certain Craig Forest: a parole violation, driving without a license, and two burglaries. The burglary warrants were really good ones because they had found his fingerprints on a shotgun he had stolen.

Putting down the phone, I told him about the four warrants. The weather was still chilly out but he immediately began to perspire. "I don't want to go back to jail," he whined. "I've only been out of jail three months now from a previous burglary arrest."

"Look, Craig," I began. "The best thing to do is let me take you down to the jail and book you. Then I'll go back and talk to the judge. When he finds out that you really want help, he'll release you to enter our program."

"Oh, no!" he shouted, rising from the chair as if to leave. "I'm not going back to jail. I'll run first!"

"No! No! God can do miraculous things for you,"

I said, motioning for him to sit down again. I remembered the numerous fellows I had gotten out of jail in New York City; sometimes ones who were already tried and sentenced. I had batted one hundred percent out there. And now that I was a cop I felt that I knew my way around even more. "Craig, there was once a man named Daniel who was sentenced to a fate worse than jail by a king much stronger than any judge here in Minneapolis. And there was no parole for stay of sentence there; so God just shut the lions' mouths."

"Look," he interrupted. "I need more than a fairy tale. These detectives have found my fingerprints. I'll be sent up for twenty years."

I promptly began to tell him the story of Israel's escape from Egypt. "God covered the evidence of their presence by a cloud," I continued. I wanted to encourage him to expect God to do miracles right from the beginning. "When the cloud of God came between the Egyptian army and those being pursued, the Israelites couldn't even be seen."

"I've never been to church," he retorted. "And I don't believe that stuff."

"All right, I'll call the chief of police and see if he'll talk to the judge so you can stay here."

A few minutes later I was talking with Chief Johnson on the telephone. I told him the four-warrant story and added that the court would make them stick because he was guilty.

The chief started laughing. "Do you know what you're asking, Palmquist? Some people are already saying our detectives couldn't find a bloody elephant in a fresh snowfall. And now you want me to give you a bloody mammoth! Good grief! This is ridiculous. I told you to call me if you needed help, but this one I don't think I can perform."

I began to feel my heart sink. Then he laughed again. "Stay there though, and I'll call you back."

Twenty minutes later he called back. "Palmquist, you tell that guy that he had better keep his nose clean. The judge gave me the four warrants to hold for future reference. If he does well, he'll be put on probation. If he goofs up, I'll be out there to deal with the situation myself."

As I put down the phone. I looked up slowly at Craig. "Guess what, Craig?" I asked. "You're home free!"

"What does that mean?" He obviously wasn't ready to admit the possibility that God might have influenced this situation in his favor.

I took a few more minutes to spell things out to him and concluded by telling him he'd never have to go back to prison as long as he did well.

He paused a few seconds, his expression stone cold. "Man, this is unreal," he said. "I've been running from cops for over ten years. You mean you are actually going to help me?" Tears trickled down his cheeks. He had been a drug user for nine years and was now strung out on hard narcotics. "Maybe there is a God."

By this time one of the other staff fellows had finished his work, so he took Craig upstairs and searched him. After he showered, he was assigned to a bed.

John, the policeman's son who had joined us the day before, got acquainted with Craig right away and began witnessing to him. He explained what it meant to repent of sins and accept Christ as Savior. The next day Craig knelt down by his bed and did just that. For a person who never went to church or didn't believe in God, he made a quick switch, but it was for real.

For the next six months Craig had many ups and downs, but eventually his wish was granted. He was placed on parole and probation.

One day a parole officer telephoned me to find out about our program. He wanted to know how much money we charged for admission. When I mentioned that there was no money or red tape involved, he said he had a fellow he wanted to have us interview right away. The kid had been sitting in jail four weeks waiting for the welfare department to give him the necessary money to enter another rehabilitation center.

After talking with the kid, I decided he was sincere, so I signed the release papers and took him back to the center with me. On the way he kept asking questions. "Are you really a cop? What are you doing this for? Why do you give a rip about me?"

I tried to explain to him how my own life had been radically changed by an encounter with Jesus Christ. "This new life is so great," I said, "that I want other people to find the Lord too."

No sooner had we reached the house and gotten him settled into the routine than another probation officer called me saying he had a fellow sitting in jail, just waiting to enter a spiritual program.

Louie Rivera and I headed towards the prison together this time. When Louie gave his testimony, the kid was really agreeable. His father was a pastor and having been raised in a Christian home, he already knew that his only chance to get himself together again was through Christ.

Now we had four fellows in the program and three of them were originally "cop-haters." However, as time passed by they gradually mellowed. I realized that their problems connected with cops were fading away when they began to teasingly call me "super cop." To them I had a great reputation because I always acted big and tough and yet they knew my heart was with them.

This nickname gained more momentum when they found out what happened to me one night after a speaking engagement. Georgene and my wife, Gayle, accompanied me to the meeting that night and, being hungry afterwards, we decided to go to the "Leaning Tower of Pizza." Besides being a friend of the manager, I loved pizza and went there often.

Driving into the parking lot, I pulled up to the curb and got out. I take my gun with me all the time, but that night I felt clumsy wearing it, so I took it off and put it in the trunk of the car before going into the restaurant.

The place was quite crowded so we were forced to take a booth right in front of the cash register. I figured I could stand the constant ding-a-ling of the cash register opening and closing for the sake of spicy sausage pizza with plenty of motzarelli. We were sitting there enjoying a nice, leisurely snack when all of a sudden the manager ran up to our booth shouting, "We've been robbed!"

Automatically I jumped to my feet and reached for my gun. The embarrassment I felt began to creep gradually up my neck to my face in shades of pink and crimson. My friend the manager had bragged about his friend the cop, big Al, many times, but when he needed me, I wasn't even prepared.

I did get my gun out of the trunk though and look around, but it was too late. The cash register had been in plain sight and the robber had even pointed a gun at the manager, but no one had noticed the smooth operation.

As we headed home that night I was surely hoping no one on the force would hear about this. I didn't exactly fit the image of "super cop."

Although we had begun a routine daily schedule at the center, the place was still a mess. During the mornings the fellows attended classes and after lunch we continued to clean, remodel, and paint.

A short while after we opened Midwest Challenge, the Minneapolis Health Inspector visited us. He was particularly interested in our kitchen. After he left, I seriously wondered if we had purchased the right house. According to him, the only thing we could leave in the kitchen was the dishwasher. Everything else had to be changed—a new ceiling, new walls (all washable), a new floor, new sink, and a new refrigerator. He could just as well have said go spend $10,000 and get a good kitchen, because that's how much we would need to comply with the order.

For several days I pondered our latest challenge. Then one day while walking through the halls down at City Hall, I decided to go in and see Sergeant Suek who had recently been promoted to lieutenant.

"Hey, I heard you're looking for a carpenter," said Suek, as I pulled up a chair to chat.

"Yeah," I grinned. "That and $10,000."

"If you can arrange it with the mayor, Palmquist, I'll be glad to come out and help remodel for a few months," he suggested.

I thought it was a great idea, so I went to the chief the same day and asked him about the possibility. Luckily, through a freak accident, there was one too many lieutenants on the force at this time and, since Suek was most recently promoted, they didn't know where to put him.

By May Suek had started working at the center, completely remodeling the kitchen and turning the attic into a recreation room. When I talked to Harland about funds, he suggested I open a charge account at the lumberyard and trust the Lord to keep it current, which He did. Every time our bills came due, we had just enough money to pay them.

Lieutenant Suek was a real asset to our program. In the morning the fellows still attended Bible classes and after lunch they worked with Suek. One of the "cop haters" had known Suek before because the lieutenant had arrested him several times.

At first the fellows were very cautious around him, but the more they got to know him, the more they loved him. He was so patient. In spite of his conscientious guidance and instruction, the fellows still made mistakes and sometimes messed things up good, but he never screamed at them or implied that they were stupid.

During the time that the remodeling was in progress, we weren't advertising for people in any way, but in July, Mike Muhar telephoned from Brainerd State Hospital Drug Ward asking if he could enter Midwest Challenge. Mike had been a childhood friend of our assistant director, Dick Harden.

I told Mike we were still developing our program and remodeling the center, but if he wanted to come down we'd pick him up at the bus depot.

When I met Mike I saw how utterly pathetic he looked. I had seen several people in New York City who had been classified as criminally insane, but I thought Mike looked worse. He seemed so depressed and unbalanced. Anything that was said had to be repeated several times before he could comprehend. He seemed to be walking around in a fog all the time. When Harland Erickson saw him in the bank with me one day, he thought I was leading a mentally retarded person around.

It wasn't long before we realized that his emotional growth had been severely stunted. Due to a congenital defect, Mike had only one arm. Naturally he had felt unaccepted from the time he was young. However, when some friends suggested he use drugs to gain acceptance and charisma, he jumped at the chance. He ended up trying everything that was available, only to realize that drugs had just the opposite effect from what his pseudo-friends had promised.

After being at the center for a while, his mind began to clear little by little. When he entered he had asked God to take over and change his life. Although his spiritual condition changed overnight, it took quite a while to develop new character traits and physical work habits.

When he first began to help paint the center, he'd get a quart of paint on the wall and a gallon on himself. One day while painting the kitchen, he turned out as green as the wall. Eventually Mike got a job working nights in a metal-plating factory. He soon saw that all the other workers would go out after work and get high, so he quit this job and enrolled at St. Paul Bible College, where he is doing well.

While at Brainerd State Hospital, he had been told that he would never be able to go to school again or use his mind fully because of all the LSD he had used. But after he began memorizing scripture, even the flashbacks from LSD stopped. Now Mike has one aim in life—to work with handicapped children. He feels he can relate better to them since he himself is handicapped.

During that first summer things were really going well for us at the center. We were excited and having fun. So much so that the day we finished painting the kitchen, Georgene and I decided to have a paint fight. Well, at least we decided after my hand accidentally got in the way of her paint brush. My hand was such a delicate green that I turned around and painted her face a pretty hue. Then she flipped a brush in my face and the chase began—up and down the stairs, back through the hall and outside. I was the final victor, having painted her face, neck, back, and both arms.

When September arrived, we began receiving more requests for high school drug programs again. I was encouraged about this aspect of the work, for we now had several people who had been freed from drugs and were making enough progress to be reliable for testimonies. Georgene, John, Craig, and Mike were willing to speak to others and had lives to back up what they said.

During one of these meetings, we made use of a brick of marijuana. The instructor said that there was a bunch of kids always hanging around the building. They had been troublemakers and expelled from school. Usually they hung around the parking lot or play area. They happened to be there that day; so the teacher took the brick of marijuana and held it out the window, yelling, "Hey! Look what I've got, you guys."

Within seconds they had bolted up the stairs and were standing in the doorway. We asked them to come in and listen while we showed a movie. It was obvious that many of them were really messed up.

After the movie Georgene told them how she

had messed around with drugs and sex until one day she had met someone that truly loved her— Jesus Christ. Georgene seemed to be reciting their own story, and many of them began to cry. Afterwards she talked with several of them who admitted they were wrong, but yet they weren't willing to give up their habit.

Late one evening in September, Gayle and I were lounging on the couch, watching television, when the phone rang. It was Jim Robertson on the other end. "Hello, Palmquist?" he began. "This is Robertson. I want you to get downtown to the chief's office right away. He may need you. Lieutenant Suek has just been shot and killed in a holdup. You'd better get Chaplain Owen too. No policemen are allowed off duty. There's a house-to-house search on to find the killer."

I just stood there for a while, dumbfounded. I could have believed it had it been any other guy except Suek. But he was always so professional and careful.

"What happened?" I asked, trying to choke back the tears.

"He was in uniform but working off-duty in a liquor store," Jim answered. "Three guys came in and staged a holdup. One of them put a gun on Suek and Suek started wrestling with him. The gun went off and shot him right through the heart."

I felt like screaming as the tears trickled down my face. "I'll get John and we'll be there in just a bit," I concluded. Hanging up the phone, I turned towards Gayle who had been staring inquisitively at me.

"Lieutenant Suek has just been shot and killed," I told her. "Call Chaplain Owen and tell him to get over here on the double. I'll get out of my pajamas and put on some clothes."

By the time John and I arrived at the chief's office, the chief and the Catholic priest had already informed Mrs. Suek of the tragedy, so we weren't needed. Instead, we joined the search. The whole force worked until 4:00 a.m. the next morning but found no one.

The next day Craig, who had finished the program, told me he had an idea who might have done it because he knew how the other guys operated. He felt the description was similar to a fellow he knew. I sent him down to see the detectives investigating the case. They searched the files for a mug shot of the guy whom Craig had mentioned and asked the store owner to look at it. He made a positive identification and the search continued.

The funeral was at Visitation Catholic Church on 45th and Lyndale. Policemen and highway patrol officers from all over the state were there. As I sat in the dark shadows of the church listening to the eulogy, I began to reminisce. Suek had taught me a lot. He was always able to scrutinize a situation and come up with an answer.

One time he had been training a young officer. While cruising around Lake of the Isles, they noticed a long-haired man washing his hair in the lake. Suek stopped the car and called the guy over to the car.

"Why don't you go home and wash your hair instead of getting our lake all dirty?" he asked.

The guy just looked up at Suek and let out a stream of profanity.

The younger officer wasn't about to let anyone talk to his supervisor that way, so in the heat of his zeal he jumped out of the squad car, knocked him down and handcuffed him. "You're under arrest," he barked.

After they had started downtown, Suek noticed

that the rookie was getting progressively more nervous. Finally, he turned to Suek and asked frantically, "Hey, what are we going to arrest him for?"

"That's simple," he replied. "Anyone that talks to us that way has got to be drunk."

I'm not sure if he was actually drunk or not, but he pleaded guilty anyway.

Suek always seemed to know if a cop had been working or just messing around on the job. That made a lot of guys nervous, especially those who were slightly lazy. Of course, he needled those of us who worked hard also.

There was one rule in the department that I managed to avoid. It says, "Whenever a policeman is outside of the squad car and in uniform, he is to wear the regulation hat."

One night my partner, Don, and I had been in a chase. We finally caught the guy at Lyndale Avenue and Lake Street by crossing over the yellow line from the left lane into the right, cutting him off as we swung the squad car in front of his. Jumping out, I ran over to his car, yanked him out and handcuffed him. Just as we were completing our fantastic piece of police work, Suek came around the corner. Traffic was jammed up all over and more cars were squealing to a halt.

In the midst of all the confusion, Suek walked over to me and said, "Palmquist, I'm concerned about you. If you don't wear your hat, you'll catch cold. I don't want to attend your funeral when you die of pneumonia." He may have been satisfied with our performance in the line of duty but would never forget my one little infraction of the rules.

Another thing he prided himself in was finding guys who had taken a few minutes' shuteye while on duty. He had caught most of the offenders except Don and me. We had a certain spot that we went to when the weather got so cold that all the crooks stayed home. It was a wooded area well out of the way.

After snoozing a bit one cold night in our hideout, we drove back to the precinct house in the morning, never thinking to check the squad car. As we drove up another officer came out. He stood there looking at the squad car shaking his head from side to side. "Suek has been looking for you guys," he warned. "Before you go into the precinct though, why don't you cut the hedges around your car?"

Quickly we jumped out of the car. Twigs and leaves hung on the hood, while assorted weeds and underbrush were enmeshed in the grill, caught on the door, and sticking out from under the wheel wells. Madly we began to strip off the foliage, dumping it into the gutter. Afterwards we walked into the precinct house only to have Suek ask, "Well, did you have a nice nap, guys?"

I never did know if he was just making a super guess or had actually seen us. Whichever it was I never doubted his ability to size up another's personality. He knew me quite well.

One afternoon a call came out over the radio stating that an Indian approximately twenty-five years old had just tried to pass a bad check at a market on 29th and Nicollet. They gave the name of the company from which the check had been issued saying it had been burglarized earlier that morning and several checks were missing. When we arrived at the store, the manager was standing outside. He described the fellow, what he was wearing, and which way he had gone.

We took off in that direction and found the guy about two blocks away, walking briskly down the street. Pulling up to the curb, I yelled, "Come here!" As soon as he reached the squad car I got out.

"You're under arrest!" I said, snapping the handcuffs on his left hand. "Where are the checks?"

He reached into his breast pocket with his free hand and gave them to me. After we got him into the back seat Don read him his rights.

"You're a really clever guy," I said, talking to him through the screen that separated us. "I just can't figure out how you got into the building this morning. It's got so many good locks." I could tell he was enjoying every minute of our one-sided conversation, so I kept complimenting him. "Do you think you could tell me how you got in there?" I continued. "I just can't figure out how you did it."

He proceeded to tell me that he had found a ladder in the alley and had used it while prying open a little window next to the door. He then reached around and picked the lock from inside. By this time he was getting very enthused about his unique ability.

"Oh, I've committed a lot of burglaries," he admitted proudly. "This was one of my easier ones."

Turning to Don, I said, "Quick! Read him his rights again, so he knows what he's getting into." He continued to brag about his escapades while I sat in the front seat, writing as fast as possible.

On the way downtown he told me about five other burglaries. After a while I began to feel like a priest in the confessional instead of a policeman. When we got to jail, he was booked and I handed in my report.

Later on I saw Suek and decided to tell him about the great confession I had gotten and how tactful I had been. Suek looked at me and laughed. "Man, you don't know nothing about getting a sophisticated confession. You probably stood on his head while twisting his arm." He turned and walked down the hall, laughing to himself. Sometimes he was joking and then again he dropped gentle hints to be careful of certain tendencies in our disposition that could give us trouble.

My reminiscing came to a halt when I heard gentle sobbing around me. The "cop-haters" from Midwest Challenge, especially Craig who had been a drug addict for so many years and whom Suek had arrested several times, were sitting alongside of me, crying like babies. I was sure this was the first time a bunch of ex-addicts had cried at a cop's funeral. They had really loved Suek, and he had felt the same about them. His wife told me at the funeral that he always talked about the center enthusiastically because he could daily see the changes in lives, especially since he had known some of them before they became Christians.

A few days after the funeral the guy who shot and killed Suek was apprehended. He had been a drug addict for many years. It seemed rather ironic that Lieutenant Suek should have spent the last five months of his life helping drug addicts and then end up being killed by one of them.

After the funeral the fellows were quite upset but not bitter. They seemed satisfied that Suek's relationship with God had been enriched while working at the center and that now he was with Christ, for whom he had done such great things through Midwest Challenge.

CHAPTER XI

During that first summer I began to get many indications from the Lord concerning our future plans and development. It was late June of 1972 when Quint Alfors stopped by the center one morning to discuss a problem with me.

The director of the Heavy Waters Coffee House had resigned and, since it had been under the auspices of the Greater Minneapolis Association of Evangelicals (GMAE), it was Quint's responsibility to find someone to replace him. As he told me about his dilemma, I just looked up and chuckled.

"Good," I said. "I've been feeling that God wanted us involved with that place." I had been there before and had appreciated the work that was being done. However, since I had worked at Teen Challenge Coffee House in Greenwich Village, New York City, I naturally made comparisons and felt that there were a few things that could be improved upon. I also figured that if Midwest Challenge could get involved with the coffee house some way, we'd have many more contacts and potential "people problems" for our program.

The few times I had been there previously, I had noticed that a good percentage of the kids who sat listening to the music were high on drugs. If we could get them interested in Midwest Challenge before they got picked up by the police or ended up in some other institution, we could avoid a lot of court pressure and red tape.

The coffee house was closed down during the month of July while Quint and I looked for a new director. Finally, we decided that the Midwest Challenge staff would operate the coffee house while the GMAE would continue to support it financially.

In August we reopened the coffee house and changed the name from "Heavy Waters" to "Logos." Our first project was to remodel and decorate it a bit. We wanted the place to be contemporary, yet in good taste. But most of all we wanted the surroundings to glorify God, to be conducive to a mind which might possibly be seeking knowledge of God.

The coffee house consists of two levels, each 30 feet by 150 feet. Our main assembly room is on the first floor as you enter the building, so we began by giving the walls of this room a fresh coat of black and white paint—black on the bottom half and white on the top. Then we scattered various colored hanging lamps around the room. It gave the impression of ladybugs dangling at the end of a spider's rope. The wooden tables which had been made from cable spools were covered with red and white checked tablecloths, and numerous colorful posters were hung on the walls.

At the back of this room is a kitchen and an office. To the right is a stairway that leads downstairs where two small carpeted rooms are used for prayer. Another room is used as a bookshop, and the remaining space has been made into a living room where people can converse more privately.

Although we officially opened the Logos in August, we spent a lot of time experimenting and shifting around. For this reason the coffee house didn't get a good start until the late fall. However, new kids kept showing up, and each week as we built relationships and friendships with people, new people turned their lives over to Christ.

It wasn't long before the Logos became an intricate part of the Midwest Challenge work. Over half of the staff works there Friday and Saturday nights, sharing the message about a Christ who gives and who changes, One who not only delivers them from drugs, alcohol, and other forms of sin, but also gives abundant life in its place.

Although we aren't running an entertainment center, we do supply special music each night in the form of folk groups and Christian rock groups. We don't mind loud or joyful music but only use groups whose basic motive is to turn someone's thoughts toward God and the salvation He has prepared through Jesus Christ.

Cookies, doughnuts, and coffee are served throughout the evening. The sign at the entrance says, "50¢ if you have it."

One of the fellows who came to the Logos in December was Tony, a Catholic fellow from Rock Island, Illinois. Tony had attended parochial school for thirteen years. He had started getting high on alcohol when he was twelve years old. Out of curiosity he began using "pot" when he was fourteen. During his first couple of years in high school, he used anything he could get his hands on and in so doing he graduated from marijuana to LSD, speed, and cocaine. He was still afraid to fool around with heroin though.

After graduating from high school, Tony joined

the army. During this time he made his first tour of duty in Viet Nam. At that time it was possible to buy a whole sandbag full of marijuana for five dollars, so he stayed high every day for a whole year. Before beginning his second year in Viet Nam, Tony returned to the States where he began snorting heroin. By the time he had returned to Viet Nam, the hashish had vanished, and now it was possible to buy three hundred dollars worth of 95% black market heroin for two dollars.

During this second year of duty Tony was a sergeant in a company of two hundred fifty men. One hundred seventy-five were strung out on heroin.

Several times he went to the army hospital, hoping to kick this habit, but each time he went right back to heroin. It was everywhere. He never lasted more than one day without it.

On the plane home from Viet Nam he and many of the other fellows were sick since their dope supply had been left behind. Luckily, however, in their opinion, the bus driver who met them at the airport landing strip stateside was selling mescaline and cocaine, so he supplied everyone, and Tony's problem continued to get worse.

Believing that LSD would help him get rid of his heroin habit, he got completely "stoned." For six days he was high and didn't sleep. After these six days he felt he could live without heroin and proceeded to do so until one day he got a letter from a buddy of his in Viet Nam. Inside the letter was a vial of heroin.

That little vial was the beginning of the end. Never again was Tony able to gain the high he was seeking. Although he mixed everything he could think of and then ate it or "shot up," he continued to get more depressed and introspective. Finally one day, after he had lost his job, all his earthly possessions, including his money, he turned to his parents for help.

His father, himself an alcoholic, suggested he enter a private hospital in Minnesota. At first the institution said there was no room available for at least a week. Then just as Tony began walking out the front door of his parents' home feeling completely crazy, the hospital called back and said they had found an empty bed.

Within the day Tony and his father had driven from Illinois to Minnesota where Tony was admitted as a patient in a private hospital.

The second day he was put in detoxification. The nurse asked him how much time had passed since he spent three consecutive days in which he was not high. When he thought back he realized it had been more than five years before. This was the first time he really got scared. All the time he had spent in Viet Nam, near death, in and out of close calls, hadn't bothered him nearly as much as the realization that he was killing himself with drugs and alcohol.

After this the nurse gave him a book which contained the twelve steps of Alcoholic Anonymous. As he looked it over that same night, the third rule made an impression on him: "We must make the decision to turn over our will and life to the care of God as we understand Him to be."

The trouble was that he didn't understand Him at all. Who was He or what was He? Tony knew that he didn't have any type of relationship with God. He had also forgotten how to pray. So he simply said, "God, if you help me to get over this, you can have my life."

During the next thirty days Tony realized that

the basic motivation of his life was gradually being changed. When he was discharged from the hospital, the doctors suggested that he go to a halfway house. So he joined a group called Progress Valley.

Their motto was living and working toward recovery. His unit consisted of twenty-one guys: five lawyers, two doctors, two psychiatrists, one pharmacist, and several professional businessmen.

Five nights a week their group therapy centered around the twelve steps of Alcoholics Anonymous. Daily Tony prayed to God as he understood Him, but he could only remember the story of the Prodigal Son; so he thought of God as an old man with a long white beard and white hair. God was always sitting in a chair and Tony called him Father.

After seven and a half months of this, Tony was "straight." He had a job, a girl friend, and was paying rent. The motto in A.A. is this, "If you aren't happy, act as if you are, and if you don't believe in God, act as if you do." Tony was acting, but deep down inside he was miserable. His thinking began to change. "If this is all there is to it," he said to himself, "I might as well go get high again."

He was weighing the pros and cons of this thought one Friday night as he walked past the Logos Coffee House at 3010 1/2 Lyndale Avenue. Since he had nothing else to do, he decided to go in and see what it was all about. Several people sat down next to Tony and began sharing about Jesus. He first thought they were nuts, never having heard anything like this before, but he soon realized that they had more than he did.

They kept asking him if he was happy, unknowingly hitting the one remaining sore spot. They encouraged him to get to know Christ in a personal way. He had never read the Bible through, so this, too, sounded crazy to him. After all, hadn't Christ died nearly two thousand years ago?

Near the end of the evening Tony couldn't argue with the fact that they were happy and he wasn't, so he went downstairs to the prayer room and even though skeptical, prayed a simple prayer. He confessed his sins and asked for forgiveness. After committing the rest of his life to Christ, he stood up, not knowing what to think. This was the first time that he felt good about God. He felt very warm inside except for the thought that maybe this feeling would go away by the next day.

That night he went to bed as usual. Early the next morning he attended a meeting. After returning to his room he noticed that his bed sheets were smooth and wrinkle-free. He had rushed out of the room in a hurry earlier that morning, not bothering to make the bed. Now his bed looked as if no one had slept in it, let alone tossing and turning all night as he usually did. It was then that he first believed that God had really done something for him.

He returned to the coffee house that night and also began attending a Tuesday night Bible study group at the Logos. After about a month of this, his friends at the halfway house began telling him he'd go nuts with all this Christianity stuff. In Tony's opinion, however, they kept contradicting themselves. One minute they were cursing and carrying on, and two seconds later they would ask him to join them in the Lord's Prayer.

Tony continued to go to group therapy where he mentioned his feelings of guilt from sin. "Look, Tony," said the psychologist, "you're too rigid. Everything is either black or white to you. You've got to learn to live in the gray areas."

147

One and a half months after Tony accepted Christ, I asked him to work weekends at the coffee house. I knew from Tony's past experience that he'd be able to empathize with other sinners and yet give a clear, sharp testimony against sin itself.

One of the last habits Tony got rid of was smoking. While still living at Progress Valley, he felt he should give up smoking for the sake of his witness. Since there were twenty-five fellows in his unit, it was 24-1 in favor of smoking, and they did it continually. Several times he tried to give up smoking but never lasted more than one day.

Then one day someone gave him a copy of Kathryn Kuhlman's book, *I Believe in Miracles*. There he read that the Bible says that if we ask anything in Christ's name, He will give it to us.

Tony had smoked since he was twelve years old. He was so dependent on cigarettes that he felt physically sick without them, "Lord," he prayed, "you know the urges I have to smoke. I claim healing and thank you for delivering me."

Then he went to work, gave his last pack of cigarettes to a fellow worker and said, "Jesus healed me, Butch. I won't be needing these anymore."

The other fellow laughed, but it wasn't long before he and several of the others at the halfway house realized that Tony was telling the truth. Tony was changing from a "caterpillar" to a beautiful "butterfly" right in front of their eyes.

Tony suddenly became aware of the change himself. The first thing he had done every morning of his life since the time he was twelve years old was to light up a cigarette. Now three weeks later he suddenly realized that he hadn't even been conscious of cigarettes for several weeks.

One of the fellows who had been watching Tony

closely was his roommate Don. Don was twenty-seven years old. He had been a thief and a part-time bartender. He was addicted to any drug he could get his hands on.

While Tony was at the halfway house, Don had watched Tony change. As a result he went to the Logos Coffee House also and accepted Christ as his personal Savior.

Another fellow who lived in the same apartment complex as Tony and Don was also watching. His name was Steve. Steve was twenty-six years old and strung on speed, mainly. He had grown up in a small farm town in southern Minnesota. He started drinking in high school and then progressed to drugs. Finally, he was "busted" for selling drugs.

When he got out of jail he committed himself to a state hospital and from there progressed to the same halfway house as Don and Tony. The first time Steve came to the coffee house he also committed his life to Christ. After getting acquainted with these fellows, I gradually noticed the struggle they were going through, being torn between two philosophies. They also felt a desperate need for Christian fellowship, so I told them they were welcome to join us at Midwest Challenge for further fellowship and teaching if they wanted to come. All three jumped at the chance, and we began to feel the expansion pains of a growing family.

Tony had been working at the coffee house for a while when Kenny, a forty-two-year-old drunk, came in and sat down. There is a bar a couple of doors down from the coffee house, and sometimes the drunks make a mistake and enter the Logos instead of the bar. It was closing time, about 1 a.m., when Kenny sat down, head in hands, but Tony took time to go over and talk with him.

Looking up, he said, "I'm just so lonely." Kenny had been a plumbing and heating contractor in a small town. His wife left him for another man and managed to take the home along with her. As a result, Kenny hit the bottle.

As Tony looked him over he realized that he had never seen an alcoholic in such bad shape. He was on the verge of death—less than skin and bones. All his teeth were rotted and the infection had spread into the facial tissues and various cavities in his head.

For quite a while Tony shared his own experiences with Kenny, emphasizing how Jesus Christ had changed his life. Tony kept promising him that everything would be different if he became a Christian; so after he prayed with him, he brought Kenny back to the center for the night. All the way back he kept saying, "I just don't know why I went into that place."

The next morning we took him down to the New Hope Center, where he stayed for several months. He was sick most of this time and very withdrawn. Every time Tony went to see him, he stuck out his hand to shake hands but turned his face away. Never once would he look Tony in the face.

One night about seven months after he first wandered into the coffee house, Kenny came to the center smiling. He had undergone such a change that Tony hardly recognized him. He had had trouble believing the Gospel until one day while lying in bed God spoke to him through His Word, proving His own reality. As a result, both his spirit and his body were healed. The transformation was fantastic. He had never had therapy, A.A., or anything else except an encounter with Jesus Christ.

Kenny asked to stay overnight at the center

again so that he could go to St. Paul in the morning. We didn't know why he wanted to go there, but we took him to the bus stop anyway. Two months later he returned. He had gone to his hometown to try to make it on his own, but he had gotten too depressed. He felt he needed a chance to mature spiritually, so he entered Midwest Challenge. Now his time is divided between his job as assistant foreman at Central Mailing Service, a business we bought through the Midwest Challenge corporation, and studying the Bible. His constant desire is to someday be a pastor.

So many young people with no previous church affiliation had been helped through the coffee house ministry that it soon became necessary to provide some means whereby they could grow spiritually. For this reason, Paul Sunde, the first coffee house director, began a Tuesday night Bible study at the Logos for those who had accepted Christ as their Savior.

At first the attendance was small, sometimes as few as three people, but Paul, who was a missionary's son and had lived most of his life in Japan, had real determination. His father, who had been a missionary for twenty years, had given him good advice: "Stick to it." And Paul did. Eventually the Bible study group enlarged so much that they had to move from the coffee house to the center.

Anywhere from thirty to one hundred people may attend these meetings, which consist of singing, sharing, praying, Bible reading, and discussion.

Recently, under the new direction of Terry Dugan, the group has begun giving towards the support of their first missionary and leader, Paul Sunde, who has gone back to Japan. This, to me, is an indication that they understand the purpose of salvation. These kids know that it's not enough to stop at getting their own lives straightened out. They have an obligation to share this new-found joy and satisfaction with others who have never heard about God's power to change and transform lives.

These others, however, do not just live in foreign countries. Many times people from the areas surrounding Minneapolis come to visit a Tuesday night Bible study at the center. One night a Lutheran ladies club attended the meeting. Terry was not able to attend that evening, so he asked Tony, Mark, and Bill to lead the service.

Bill had been one of these fellows who had started using cocaine and speed at the age of fourteen or fifteen years. He was twenty-six years old, though, when he wandered into the center one day high on cocaine and looking for thirty dollars. He had gone to a pastor he knew to ask him for the money. The pastor in turn sent him to Midwest Challenge—Bill thought for money, but the pastor had meant for help.

His hair was down to his shoulders, his beard was full grown, and he literally stank, his ragged clothes half falling off his body.

Now, about four months later, he stood before a group of twenty-five sophisticated women, completely at ease. God had not only changed his heart attitude and condition, but his life-style had also been radically changed. Now it was mighty difficult to find him in anything less than a sport coat.

After praying that God's presence would fill their hearts and minds, he turned the meeting over to Mark, a tall nineteen-year-old blond who had used everything from "pot" to heroin.

His mother had taken him from one psychiatrist to another, only to find that he got progressively worse. After hearing about Midwest Challenge from her boss at work, Mark's mother arranged an interview for him. We accepted him into the program and began to pray that God would get hold of his mind as well as his heart.

The first week he was very withdrawn and sullen, so I decided he maybe could use a change of scenery. The following week I took him along to a church banquet at which I was guest speaker. While I was speaking I noticed that Mark was acting strangely, so when he got up and walked out of the building, I motioned for Tony to follow him.

Turning around, he spoke to Tony. "Tony, I feel like I'm going to get sick. There's such a strong taste of sulphur in my mouth. I think it's a demon." He continued telling Tony about a certain dream he kept having. In this dream there was a white horse and a black horse facing each other as if for war, and Mark sat simultaneously on both horses. Tony felt it was a battle for his spirit because Mark had been involved with the occult through brotherhood drugs. These are drugs supposedly blessed by the devil.

Tony quickly went back to the banquet hall and got another staff member to come with him back to the parking lot. Together they prayed for Mark, asking God to erase this dream from Mark's memory and to free him from any effects incurred while involved in the occult.

Instantly there was a noticeable change in his personality. He turned his life over to Christ that very night and continued allowing God to remake his character in the likeness of God's special example, Jesus. The next time his mother came to see him she was amazed. "I don't even know him," she said. "He's a new person."

Now, as he stood before the women's group giving his testimony, it was obvious that he was no longer bound by Satan. "I feel so free in Christ," he said, after describing the change in his life. "You just don't know the difference."

As he spoke, one of the ladies began to cry. When he was finished, she stood up in front of the other ladies and said that two years ago she had accepted Christ into her life, but she had never made it public until now. When she sat down, Tony began to explain a bit more about the Christian's responsibility to share this message of hope with others.

Instantly one of the other women raised her hand and said, "Our Lutheran heritage teaches us that we aren't to go out and witness but just be good examples."

"It's very necessary to be a good example," answered Tony, "but Matthew 10:32 also says, 'If anyone publicly acknowledges me as his friend, I will openly acknowledge him as my friend before my Father in heaven.' I think both aspects are necessary."

Then another hand went up in the air. "What do you mean by 'accepting Christ'?" another woman asked.

"I was a Catholic all my life," began Tony. "I knew about the life of Jesus and believed that He was the Son of God, but it wasn't until I realized what wanting my own way was all about that I understood the importance of Christ's death on the cross. If all I agreed to in my mind concerning Christ was true, then I was morally obligated to thank Him by giving Him whatever was left of my remaining life to do with as He pleased. If any of you ladies really believe what the Bible says about Christ taking your place on the cross, we would be glad to pray with you."

After the service that night, two members of the

group did decide to change their life-style by letting God into the "driver's seat."

As they walked out the door, the chairman of the group spoke to Tony. "Tony, before we came tonight I had difficulty raising $25 to give to your cause. I guess the ladies just weren't willing. But since coming to the meeting, they have offered $60 to be used in giving others another chance in life."

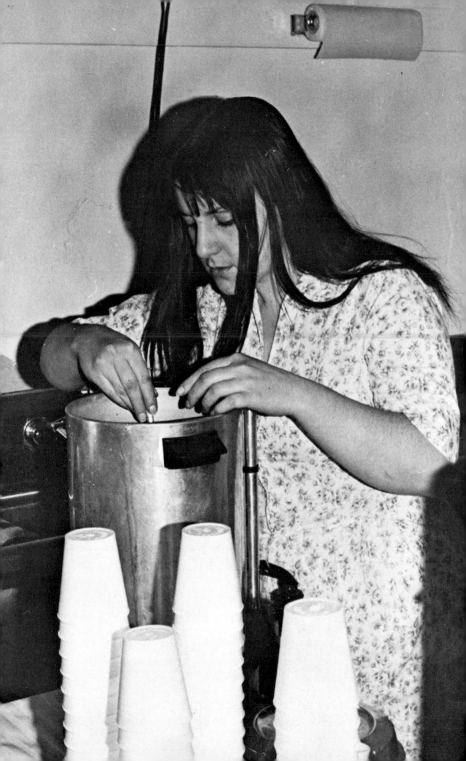

CHAPTER XII

Shortly after we finished remodeling the center on Columbus Avenue, several girls came to the door, asking if they could enter the program. They obviously needed help, but the Health Department had said we could house only boys in the place.

As a result, I started looking for another place to use for a girls' program. I didn't have any great revelation from God to lead me on, but I did know there was nothing chauvinistic about God. He is just as concerned about the happiness and well-being of women as He is of men. The more I looked, however, the more I seemed to run into a dead-end street. Everything I saw was unsuitable.

One day as I sat in my office praying about this problem, I received a telephone call from a pastor's wife in a suburban Presbyterian church. I had met her at a meeting before, but she introduced herself again anyway. Then she began to tell me that for several days during her prayer time she had been seeing my face. And, now she wondered why she was calling me.

About that time, I felt like Daniel must have felt when the king asked him to interpret his dream. She not only wanted me to interpret her vision, but she wanted me to tell her what it was. But, unlike Daniel, I just grabbed at the first thing that came to mind.

"Does your church have a nice house you're not using that you'd like to give to us?" I asked.

"Yes! That's it!" she replied. "We have a house right next to the church. It's a nice three-bedroom rambler with a large basement that could be used as a recreation room. It used to be the parsonage, but now it's empty."

My mouth hung open.

"It just has to get an O.K. from the church board and the village council," she continued.

This time my heart sank. It was bad enough that the idea had to pass two boards; but since it was located in a well-to-do suburban community, I was sure the village council would vote against having a home for delinquent female drug addicts located there.

I had momentarily forgotten who had originated this idea, however, and a short time later saw the completion of God's plan. The idea was approved by both boards, and just about a year after the opening of the boys' home we opened the girls' home at 7115 Fifth Avenue South.

A short while after we were given this home, Dale and Dianne Kallenberg, graduates of Bethany Fellowship Missionary Training Center, called me, offering to work as house parents at the girls' home. Since we needed more staff to work in this capacity and they had just completed two years of missionary service in the West Indies, I felt that they were experienced enough to handle the work.

The church then offered to remodel and furnish the house as well as to pay the Kallenbergs' salary and meet the expenses of the program.

The first girl who came for help was what is known as a "Midwestern garbage head." Some people say there are no pure drug addicts in the Midwest, meaning those who only mainline heroin. Most serious drug users in this part of the country use anything they can get their hands on. For Beverly it was amphetamines, barbiturates, LSD, and speed. She had gotten so bad that she voluntarily committed herself to the Hastings State Hospital.

When she was discharged from there, her mother sent her to us. Beverly was in the girls' home for several months. She went through the motions of accepting Christ as her Savior, but her life was really never changed. She continued to rebel at authority and constantly sought attention in bizarre ways.

During her stay at the girls' home she went horseback riding and broke her arm. Then a few weeks later while attending a "Basic Youth Conflicts" seminar, she disappeared during one of the meetings. Her counselor looked all over for her and finally found her out in the hallway, trying to saw her arm cast off with a serrated knife.

Finally, after much time counseling with her, it was obvious that she wouldn't cooperate with the program, so Dale had to dismiss her.

A month after Beverly began living with the Kallenbergs, we heard about a twenty-three-year-old girl named Donna who was confined in the Shakopee Women's House of Detention. Donna's childhood friends had visited her there in prison, telling her about a chance to start her life over with Christ. She thought it was a pretty good idea and accepted God's plan for her life while still in jail.

When we heard about her, she was up for parole. Her parole officer had suggested that she go to a halfway house, mentioning several possibilities. She refused her suggestions, however, because she wanted to enter a spiritual program. She wrote to Teen Challenge on the East Coast, but her parole board would not let her go out of state. It was during this time that someone turned her name in to Midwest Challenge.

One of our staff members went to visit her immediately. She was thrilled. She had never imagined there was a spiritual program located in Minneapolis. Within days her parole board had given her permission to leave prison and enter the Midwest Challenge Girls' Home.

Donna had never lived in one place more than three months at a time during the previous six years. Now that she was, for all practical purposes, under house arrest, she began to squirm a bit. Every girl who enters the home is first given a copy of the house rules which she must sign before being accepted. These rules include: no drugs, no smoking or drinking, no street talk, and no dating. They were allowed a small amount of spending money each week and then could go out to spend it only if they were accompanied by a staff member.

Donna, like most of the other girls who eventually entered the program, found submitting to authority the most difficult lesson to learn. However, she was really sincere about changing her life-style, so she tried to comply in all areas. Eventually she finished the program and is now working as a nurse's aide, hoping to someday enter a nurses' training program.

Nancy came to Midwest Challenge from the psych ward at Ramsey County Hospital. The doctor had suggested to her that she enter a spiritual program, since she had been involved in both drugs and Satan worship. When she was interviewed, she said she had even gone so far as to cut her own body and offer her blood to the devil.

Nancy continued to reveal bizarre stories of witch-craft and other freak accidents. She insisted that one night she and her boyfriend had been babysitting for a friend. Her boyfriend had left early to hop a train which ran along the tracks in front of the house. Later that evening she went to the store to get some milk. While walking along the train track (a shortcut to the store), she suddenly kicked into something heavy. When she bent down to see what it was, she found the body of her boyfriend who had been decapitated while trying to board the speeding train.

At first those who heard her stories were horrified by the many seemingly cruel circumstances surrounding her life. But later on everyone realized that her main problem was separating reality from imagination. Her boyfriend had never been killed, but several years earlier while still in high school, an acquaintance of hers had been killed in a train accident.

Nancy made gradual progress. Finally, she was able to admit that most of her stories were lies. However, she had been involved in worshipping Satan, the father of all lies. Shortly after she finished the program, a weird looking woman came to the door of Midwest Challenge and announced that she was a witch and intended to put a curse on the program because we had been stealing followers of Satan.

After Nancy returned to her home, her mother sent a letter to me stating that she was so thankful to have Nancy home again because she was a new girl. Since returning home, Nancy had spoken to her mother in a civil tone of voice for the first time in over six months.

Joan was in the program only one week, but it was the saddest and most frustrating week ever spent trying to help one individual. Joan had been in a mental institute for quite a while. She had begun using drugs while attending the University of Minnesota. During this time she sang in the university choir. She apparently thought she was in love with one of the directors, and when one day he spoke to the choir in general saying, "I can't get any eye contact with you. You obviously don't know the song because you're glued to the music," she blew her mind. Her whole love affair had only been one-sided and based on eye contact. After that she began wearing a veil constantly and saying she was going to marry Jesus.

Joan came to us from another halfway house. She said she was a Christian but needed to get away from this other halfway house where they kept giving her drugs.

The first day, she approached Dale every hour with some problem. She wanted to talk or be counseled constantly. The whole time she would flutter her eyelashes in a strange manner. The second evening she was sitting quietly in a chair when without warning she began to scream and laugh hysterically. The staff prayed for her for several hours and she finally settled down. But she didn't sleep more than two hours during the remainder of the week.

Each night Joan's roommate would be wakened from sleep by the same weird laughter, only to find Joan lying motionless on her bed, staring at the ceiling, her eyes fluttering strangely.

After supper one evening Dale asked Joan if she

would read from the Bible for devotions. She began reading and verse by verse her facial expression became more angry. Within minutes she was screaming and yelling vulgarly as she ran to her room.

The next day Dale was sitting at the table talking to someone else when Joan walked up to him in a serious manner and called him father.

"I'm not your father, Joan," he said. "We're friends in Christ."

Ten minutes later she approached him again and addressed him as "Daddy." Later on that afternoon when Dale bent down to give his little girl Chris a hug, Joan, who was also in the room, asked, "Why don't you do that to me?"

It didn't take long for Dale's wife to explain that to her.

By the end of the week it was obvious that she would have to be dismissed. She was a threat to the others in the house. On Friday night she was caught sneaking out of her bedroom after "lights out time." When Dale asked her what she was doing, she said she had to go to the bathroom. A short time later as Dale walked from the living room down the hall to his bedroom, he found Joan standing at his bedroom door, her head inside the door.

"What are you doing, Joan?" he asked, coming up behind her.

"I was listening to see what you and your wife were doing," she said shrugging her shoulders nonchalantly.

The next morning, as a last resort, Dale and another staff member took Joan to the home of another pastor for prayer and counseling.

"Joan, what's your problem?" asked the pastor as they sat down in his office.

"I've been molested," she retorted immediately.

"Joan, you said just the other day when I was talking to you that nothing like this had ever happened," remarked Dale, looking at her reprovingly.

"Oh, I forgot," she continued. It was obvious that she was lying. After a while it was evident that counseling wasn't worthwhile, so they began to pray for her. She then began to speak about being full of demons—lust, masturbation, homosexuality, and every other foul spirit imaginable.

It was apparent that Joan knew a lot about the Bible, but it was difficult to determine whether or not she was putting on an act.

Eventually they decided to take her back to the girls' home and dismiss her. As soon as they got into the car, she broke into convulsive laughter. When they arrived back at the center, it was three o'clock in the afternoon. Immediately she got into her pajamas and stood in front of the mirror for an hour admiring herself.

Later on someone turned the stereo on. The music was Christian but she began yelling for rock music as she frantically danced around the house. She was told no, so she began swearing and hopping around like a rabbit.

During this time Dale was trying to contact her parents without success. As he contemplated what to do next she got worse, pushing over furniture, throwing whatever she saw. Her strength was abnormal. Besides this, her language was obscene, begging for someone to take advantage of her.

After she threatened to kill her roommate, they forcibly confined her on a chair while Dale called the police. When the police arrived, she was as quiet as a purring kitten—so much so that they wondered what was going on and asked that she be untied. That was a big mistake. The purring kitten instantly became a raging tiger. She tore into the cops, kicking and screaming. It took four policemen to subdue her. Finally they had her pinned on the floor while they called an ambulance. She continued to bang her head on the floor as she thrashed, however, so Dale bent down to put a pillow under her head so she wouldn't hurt herself. Then she began to speak—but it wasn't her own voice. It was a strange, low, unearthly voice.

As the ambulance pulled away, everyone in the house knelt down in the kitchen and asked God to get rid of any spirit that would oppose God's Holy Spirit of peace, love, and serenity.

The girls who entered the girls' home after this were a bit more "normal," for which everyone involved was thankful. However, we all continue to pray that someday we'll be able to better help someone like Joan.

About six months after the girls' home opened, I got a telephone call from a man by the name of John Hartzell. John felt that God wanted him to work with drug addicts also, but in a special way. He was the foreman of a mailing service and had employed ex-addicts from various halfway houses around the Twin Cities. Now he wanted to know if Midwest Challenge, Inc., would be willing to buy this business and use it as a means to further train ex-addicts, enabling them to eventually return to society successfully.

Immediately my mind flashed back to the time I sat in Jim Robertson's office, working on the proposed program for Midwest Challenge. I remembered definitely stating that our ultimate goal was to become at least partially self-supporting while at the same time using this business as a means of training those who came to us. I had prayed about it at the time and then having gotten so involved with the other aspects of the work, forgot to expect God's answer. Now, as I talked to John on the telephone, I sensed that God was nudging me again.

John had been a pastor himself, working many years with young people through the Navigators and the Billy Graham Association. While working at the Graham Association, John had joined with several other men to buy a mailing service.

It was while being foreman of the shop that he first got the idea of employing drug addicts. One day there was so much work to do that he called Employers Overload and asked for ten workers.

"Do you care if they have long hair?" asked the guy at the other end of the phone.

Deep down he felt uncomfortable about the idea but said as long as they worked it didn't make any difference to him. They worked all morning and then during lunchbreak they disappeared. John wasn't sure where they had gone until the owner of the building showed up, fuming.

The owner had been showing a prospective tenant around the building. As they approached one of the offices, the owner mentioned that this would be a great room for an executive office. As he opened the door to show off the room, he was confronted by ten shabby, greasy, long-haired creatures sitting in a circle on the floor, smoking "pot."

This was John's first introduction to drug users. After being chewed out royally by the boss, he quickly informed the ten fellows that as long as they wanted to work here there would be no drugs in the building.

Eventually, one of the fellows, Tim, a doctor's son and a heavy drug user, decided to choose Christ's type of high instead of the artificial joy of drugs. John's experience with Tim encouraged him to help more drug addicts until finally he felt the best thing to do would be to merge with Midwest Challenge.

As usual we did not have sufficient cash on hand, but after negotiations, we were able to pay $800 down and begin monthly payments three months later.

About two and a half months after purchasing this mailing service, we ran out of work. We called all the staff and people in the program together for a prayer meeting. After much prayer and four telephone calls, we had enough business to last more than two months.

The business venture continues to expand so that we are bringing people from other halfway houses to work. They are being paid not only for their work but to also participate in an hour-long Bible study conducted every morning by the foreman, John Hartzell.

Each time that God has answered my prayer, He has had much larger horizons in mind than I could ever have imagined, whether it concerns a means to help drug addicts, or a way to meet the spiritual needs of people in crisis. God not only brought the Chaplaincy Corps into existence but added the chaplain work with policemen themselves.

He didn't stop with opening a center at 3045 Columbus, but He also added a girls' home and a business through which we not only supply work for our own fellows and girls but which also reaches out to the hearts of those involved in other halfway houses.

As I've watched this story unfold around me, I've come to one conclusion: God is taking ordinary Christians and encouraging them to look beyond their own preconceived ideas and limitations to explore avenues of service which may previously have seemed unapproachable.

EPILOGUE

In July of 1973 Al Palmquist spoke briefly during the Billy Graham Crusade in the Twin Cities. He mentioned how God had used him as a policeman to begin a drug rehabilitation program in Minneapolis.

This Crusade was filmed and replayed on television in November at which time a woman in Tulsa, Oklahoma, was asking God to solve a special problem. A short time earlier a young fellow from Minnesota had called her because she was the only Christian he knew. His name was Jack, and while hitchhiking around the country, using drugs, he had met her and her husband who had witnessed to him about Christ.

He telephoned from a halfway house in Minnesota, asking her if she knew of any place he could get free from drugs and straight with God. Not knowing offhand of any such place, she said she would call him back. Seconds later, switching on her television set, she saw Al's face and heard his testimony.

The next morning she called Midwest Challenge, giving Jack's name and address to Al. Within a week

Jack was attending classes and deeply involved in the program at Midwest Challenge. During one of these classes the topic of discussion was repentance and restitution. Jack was full of guilt concerning an incident that had happened in his hometown. One night he took three times the usual dose of LSD. As a result he completely "flipped out." He wandered around until finally he entered a strange home and severely beat an unsuspecting woman.

The chief of police in the town had suspected him and brought him in for her to identify, but she was unable to make a positive identification. As a result he was set free, but his conscience was still harassed.

He came to Al and asked for help. A meeting was arranged between the woman and her husband, the chief of police, the woman's doctor, and Al and Jack.

Al tried to explain to the police chief and the woman what had happened and that he hoped that Jack could stay in the program. However, they didn't seem too favorable.

When Jack came into the room, he confessed that he had done the crime and that since he had become a Christian he wanted to make things right.

"Why did you do it?" asked the woman.

Jack tried to explain what happened. As he finished, she asked, "How do I know you won't do it again?"

It was then that Jack explained to her why he was the way he was and how he had changed. He didn't blame society or his environment or any other thing in his past. He simply explained that he had been a selfish sinner with what psychologists call the "King Baby Syndrome"—I want what I want when I want it. He then shared what Christ had done for him and how His love and forgiveness had put new motivation into his life.

As he told this story, the tears began to roll. Wiping his eyes with a hanky, the woman's husband said, "Look, Jack, the only thing we're concerned about is that you stay in that program and really become a man."

After the legal implications were settled, Jack turned to the woman one more time to ask her forgiveness and to say good-bye. Grabbing him, the woman hugged him and kissed him on the cheek. "We just want everything good for you, Jack."

As the tears streamed down the cheeks of those present, God's healing baths of love and forgiveness washed away the hurt, guilt, and bitterness hidden in the depths of those people directly involved.

And once again, a situation that Satan had intended to use as a tool of destruction and depravity was turned into a means of becoming a new person through God's love.